ADAPT

ADAPT

LESSONS LEARNED CLIMBING 100 5.13'S

KRIS HAMPTON

Copyright ©2024 by Power Company Climbing

All rights reserved. No part of this book may be reproduced or utilized in any form, or by electronic, mechanical, or other means, without the prior written permission of the author.

Written and illustrated by Kris Hampton
Cover design by Kris Hampton
Cover photo by John Wesely
Edited by Lana Stigura and Kris Hampton

Power Company Climbing
Lander, Wyoming
www.powercompanyclimbing.com

Paperback ISBN: 978-1-7341036-2-5
Ebook ISBN: 978-1-7341036-3-2

DISCLAIMER
Climbing and training for climbing are inherently dangerous. Your safety depends on your own judgment. The author and any persons associated with Power Company Climbing will assume no liability for accidents or injuries sustained by readers of this book. If you are unwilling to assume all responsibility for your own safety, please do not use this book.

**Never looking back, or too far in front of me.
The present is a gift, and I just wanna be.**

– Common

CONTENTS

FOREWORD	1
NOTE FROM THE AUTHOR	7

LEARN

I'm Not a Sport Climber	13
The Goal Is to Be	17
Get Over Yourself	22
Macro Commitment	25
Preparation Affords Confidence	28
Train What Matters	30
Build Something to Stand On	33
The Art of Execution	37
Stronger Is the Wrong Answer	41
Conditions Matter, but Not as Much as You Think	43
Training Principles Don't Apply to Performance	46
The Key	50

GROW

Pressure on Purpose	57
A Good Partner Is a Great Asset	62
Shoot Smarter	65
Are You the Same You?	68

Aphorisms and Absolutes	73
Consistency Is Complicated	76
Less Isn't More	79
Science Isn't Right	80
Changing Constraints Are New Opportunities	85

EXCEL
Adapt and Go Boom!	93
Responsibly Selfish	99
Quality Control	106
Comparison Didn't Steal Anything	108
Micro Commitment	111
No Time Not To	114
It Comes Down to You	120
Fold Faster	123
It Ain't Over 'Till It's Over	128
Outcomes Matter: An Epilogue	135

COUNT TO 100	140
ACKNOWLEDGEMENTS	143
ABOUT THE AUTHOR	145

FOREWORD

By John Wesely

For the last year, I had watched the number go up.

86, 87, 88.

The goal itself was questionably arbitrary, Kris had thrown his hat over the fence and was going to bring his lifetime total of 5.13 sends to 100 by the time his age reached half that number. That's only two 13's a year if you start the day you are born, which is not too unreasonable considering what youth climbing programs are able to achieve in the year 2024. However, Kris didn't have the foresight to start climbing as an infant, and to top it off, had assumed the position of a sport-climber-in-deep-remission since moving to Lander. This foolishness meant he had fifteen 13's left to tick in the final year of his youth instead of the two he would've had if he'd just been a bit more diligent. With his work cut out for him, Kris got to it.

89, 90, 91.

I could relate to Kris's aversion to the sport climbing around town. Compared to the luxuriously textured, immaculately shaped sandstone of Kentucky's Red River Gorge – both my and Kris's home crag before shipping ourselves out West – the Bighorn Dolomite of the Wind River foothills is downright mean. Slick dime edges, angry sharp pockets, and off-balance thrutch characterize the climbing. The ever-present danger of cranking hard on one too many glassy monos adds a unique flair wholly absent from the glorious jug bashes of Eastern Kentucky. To knock off fifteen of these lil' fuckers in less than a year would be an undertaking for a kid working part-time at the Lander Bar, let alone a man rapidly approaching his golden years with a toddler in tow. So I watched with some interest.

92, 93, 94.

September had rolled in and Kris was still cooking, sinking time into both bolting new choss and appreciating the choss of old at a lesser-known crag called Miners Delight.

95, 96, 97.

One of these was a bit audacious, an abandoned project at the upper end of 5.13. Personally, if I had a week left to complete a very public goal I had set for myself, I would have been searching "softest 5.13's in Ten Sleep" on Reddit, but it is a free country. Overcoming the laws of common sense, Kris sent.

98.

With a week left, Kris switched gears and moved his focus to a neat little granite crag up in Sinks Canyon that sees evening shade called The Joint. With one day left until his 50th birthday, Kris still had two whole routes left and very little time.

I was already planning on going out that day with my buddy Sean, and easily convinced him that we should go to The Joint to help Kris try to finish this thing. My motives were not entirely selfless as climbing in a party of three meant I could take pictures, and taking pictures meant I wouldn't have to belay – a tremendous perk. Kris said he was down and had two teed up that he thought would go. After a perfunctory warmup, we hopped on the first objective, a little power tech shorty called Broken Heroes, 13a. Kris gave it strong effort but came up short near the chains. I tied in and something became quickly apparent. The air was pretty warm that day, but the rock was hot. The dark black and tan granite had been baking in the intense Wyoming sun since sunrise, and despite it being nominally October, air temps firmly in the 80s made it feel not quite like the crispy fall day you might expect.

After dogging for what seemed to be half the afternoon, I reached the anchors via a combination of desperate pawing on some WARM micro crimps and creative rope work. This was not the type of climb you wanted to be doing on a day like this. The holds which appeared to be generous incuts from the ground were deceptively flat. I would chalk up my hands, pull on the wall, and immediately feel the moisture seeping through my tips as I gripped the heat-soaked rock while ineffectually smearing my feet. Kris shared none of my excuses. He tied in and turned it on hard. Despite the suboptimal conditions, he grunted through it and got it done, squeezing the life out of every hold.

99.

With the light fading, we moved over to the final piece in this puzzle, a fresh-off-the-presses 13a called Awake and Dreaming. The meat of the climbing is in the bottom twenty feet. A full-extension crank off of a marginal sidepull leads right into the crux boulder, a devious traverse featuring a cryptic sequence topped off with an absolute shoulder-busting cross. Kris gave it a solid go, once again fully turning it on and giving *Dosage*-era Jason Kehl a run for his money in the try-hard department. Sometimes it just isn't enough, and Kris popped off right before he was through it.

Traversing the talus field back to the car via headlamp, we strategized: the deadline was tomorrow, with a forecast telling us it was going to get even hotter. It is one thing being third day on in your 20s, but a man entering his fiftieth year needs all the help he can get.

We took the only viable option, arriving at the crag pre-dawn in an attempt to catch the rock before it could soak up the sunlight and spoil any chance of success. It was a good plan.

Well, it seemed like a good plan. Even before first light, the residual heat from the previous day radiated off the rock. Racing against the sun, Kris hopped on and fell at the same crux move as the night before. The gambit didn't seem like it would play out. The sun peeked over the far side of the canyon and was racing towards the cliff as Kris gave it another solid burn, once again falling in the crux. I figured that was it. The wall was now burning in the sun. He was cooked both metaphorically and practically. He had given it an honest attempt, but there are limits to everything. Kris was running up against several of them. Conditions, fatigue, and time were now co-conspirators in the plot to tank this whole mission, but Kris had that dog in him.

He stepped off the ground and left it all on the rock. Screaming like a demon on every move, he fought for every single inch. This was it. There would be no more chances. He could put it down now or be forced to write an article about lessons learned from public failure. He eked his way through the crux and what happened next I will never forget. Kris had pushed way past the redline and his forearms were done. Mountain Project describes the 30 feet of exit climbing as merely 11+. That may well be true, but watching Kris absolutely melt off every single move to the chains was an equal mix of inspiring and hilarious. I don't know what kept him on the wall. My only guess is that the overwhelming force of the sunk cost propelled him upwards. Climbing at a glacial pace of two feet per minute, sliding off every hold, sheer will gluing him to the rock, he reached the chains.

100.

I haven't read this book yet, so I don't know what lessons Kris learned from his 100 5.13's. All I can tell you is the lesson I learned from spending the last few hours of that journey with him. If you set a big goal and put your back to the wall, you can do some pretty dope things. Could Kris have put a couple more sessions in, wired that route, and hiked it? I would hardly be surprised. Could he have dug as deep as he would have had to in order to do it third day on in the blazing sun later that day? I guess we will never know, but I would like to think there is something there. Go for it. Get invested. Put enough in that it will hurt if you lose it. You might surprise yourself.

NOTE FROM THE AUTHOR

I didn't plan to write this book. I figured I would finish my hundred 5.13's and move on to the next checkpoint goal that moves me toward the larger, more encompassing goal to become the best climber I can be.

Obviously, that's not what happened.

Instead, with the early morning sun beating on me at bolt five or six of 5.13 number 100 – the exact spot captured by John Wesely for the cover photo of this book and described in his foreword – I found myself fighting for every inch of upward progress on terrain that, by all reasonable estimations, I should have been cruising.

Not a single move felt possible the way I had practiced it. I recognized a bit of panic swelling up. My forearms were completely bricked, and for a moment, I just wanted to be done. In order to stay on, I had to pull out nearly every trick I had learned over nearly 20 years of climbing.

These climbs that we do, these goals that we choose, are valuable. They are filled with constraints that either shape our solutions or block our passage. Reflecting on that final route, sent on the morning of my 50th birthday, I realized that I'm pretty good at working within the constraints presented and finding a solution. I've been told I'm good at executing the plan when the time comes, and I suppose I'm proud of that. But on that day, I didn't execute the plan at all.

When the constraints change and my planned solution is no longer viable, I'm very good at adapting my solution instead of falling victim to blocked passage.

That's something I'm even more proud of.

I've done it over and over. Not dodging life's changing constraints but exploring them and adapting. It's a valuable skill. If, like me, your goal is to become the best climber you can be, it's the most valuable skill.

There's a story that weaves its way through these pages. A story of what constraints were in place and when, and how I dealt with them. But it's not about that narrative as much as it's about the lessons learned along the way. I hope you can see yourself in some of these stories. Or when you do find yourself boxed in by similar obstacles, which you undoubtedly will, you'll remember that there is, despite how it feels in that moment, a solution.

My climbing on the final few bolts of that route was not pretty, but I didn't let go. I calmed the rising panic. I sorted out which pieces of my original plan would still work and filled in the gaps where it wouldn't. I accepted that I might fall, but that I would fall trying my best to do one simple thing:

Adapt.

LEARN

April, 1995 — *Started climbing*

1996 — *First 5.12*

1996 — *First time climbing outside*

October, 1997 — *First daughter born*

1997-2001 — *Nearly all trad climbing, up to 5.12d*

2001-2005 — *Climbed only a few times a year*

2004 — *John Bronaugh passes away*

Late 2005 — *Returned to the climbing gym to start training*

2006 — *45 routes 5.10 and harder, including two 12a's*

2007 — *200 routes 5.10 and harder, including sixty-two 5.12's*

October, 2007 — *First 13a*

2008 — *115 routes 5.11 and harder, including eleven 5.13's*

October, 2008 — *First 13b*

2009 — *Started dedicated finger training*

May, 2009 — *First 13c*

2010 — *Fourteen 5.13's, including eleven 13b's*

April, 2011 — *Papaw passes away*

April, 2011 — *First 13d*

I'm Not a Sport Climber

It was drizzly and wet in the Red River Gorge, which is barely a concern for a sport climber. The steep walls stay dry in most downpours. But on Saturday, October 16th, 2004, I wasn't a sport climber. I had just turned 30, and though I'd built a bit of a buzz as a trad climber and climbing rapper, I hadn't actually been climbing much. Sometime around 1999 I traded my time seeking hard cracks in the Kentucky woods for the hard knocks of the underground Hip Hop scene. The more things bubbled on the mic, the less time I spent on the rock.

But I believed that I'd be able to climb 5.11 cracks forever, no matter how little time I'd spent climbing, and my friend Yasmeen Fowler who was doing her best to drag me outside as often as possible had recently been moving into the grade. So on this damp day we found ourselves at Mt. Olive Rock, where I knew a thin 11a dihedral called South Side of The Sky was capped by a massive roof and would remain dry.

I'd climbed it years earlier, so Yasmeen took the lead. She'd only led a few routes on gear at this level, none quite as insecure as this one. But she was remarkably adaptable, and as I'd learn, remarkably in control.

With only one warmup, the relatively easy intro moves required a little more struggle than I expected to see, but she soon found a stance below the mostly holdless crux. After fiddling in small gear, she launched into the strangely bouldery stemming smears and tips locks.

"Watch me Kris, I'm scared!"
A brief pause and I noticed her shoulders relax.
"No. No I'm not."

At the time, this was surprising and hilarious, but over the years I'd see Yasmeen calmly rationalize her way through many situations, on and off the wall. It's one of the many things I admire about her. But more important, she was learning something I had yet to fully embrace: adaptability.

I followed her lead, and sat wondering at the top about the wet, wide, lichen-covered crack that led out the roof from the anchors. I often wondered about these repellant monstrosities back then, sometimes allowing my wonder to give way to exploration and groveling in the pursuit of some invisible glory that came with being the first to do something nobody else had even considered. Not because they couldn't – simply because it wouldn't be at all pleasant.

Those days are long past, thank goodness.

Back on the ground, the suggestion was made to do a mostly forgotten 11a sport climb called South Central that followed a pocketed face a few steps to the right. I'm not sure if this was Yasmeen's idea or mine, but for some reason I tied in for the lead.

Now let me reiterate something: At that moment, standing beneath that sandy, 50-foot route with twilight approaching, I was *not* a sport climber. I didn't go to a climbing gym. I didn't train. I hadn't clipped bolts in many years. Hell, I only climbed a few times a year at best. I was relying entirely on crack climbing skills to get up things.

But it's 11a.

I had just done a 5.11 crack with no trouble, and everyone says sport climbing is easier and overgraded.

Everyone is wrong.

I don't remember much of the climb. I assume it went fine for the first few bolts. What I do remember is that at some point, a couple of bolts or so below the anchor, I was stopped cold. The positive pockets had disappeared. Not that it mattered – I was far too pumped to hold on to anything. In particular, I was too pumped to even begin to use the nothingness masquerading as a sloper that was blocking my way.
In my failing and deceptive memory, that sloper was the only way. And there was no way possible I was going to pass it.
Yas finished the route for me.
I'd seen many people magically grow abilities when attached to a toprope, and my hubris didn't extend to the belief that I was above that phenomenon, so I offered to go back up and clean it on toprope. But there was that sloper. And I was destined to stay below it.
In the dark, Yas finished the route for me. Again.

Oh, well. I'm not a sport climber.

I had a Hip Hop event to get to in Cincinnati, the *Battle for Midwest Supremacy*, but on the drive, being supreme at anything was the furthest thing from my mind. I could barely hold the steering wheel. My mind wandered to a statement that had been made about me by local legend, route developer and guidebook author, John Bronaugh.

> "I don't think Kris is an overachiever. I think he's an underachiever. He does just enough to get noticed and then he bails to something else."

John had been one of the early forces in exploring the traditional climbing that the Red had to offer, and one of the few who seamlessly made the switch to sport climbing. His forward-thinking acceptance of both styles made him the perfect person to document the area in guidebooks. Every route description was prose worthy of memorizing. And we did, often excitedly quoting the descriptions before embarking on an onsight attempt.

So when he wrote this about me in an online forum, I was crushed. Because he was right.

John had tragically passed away in August of 2004, shortly before my dismal attempts on South Central. My failure on the route only highlighted the accuracy of his understanding of me.

With that terrible sloper and John's words echoing in my head, a seed had been planted. It would take another year before I began to nurture that seed, but I would eventually see it grow.

I was going to become the best climber I could be.

My first step was to become a sport climber.

The Goal Is to Be

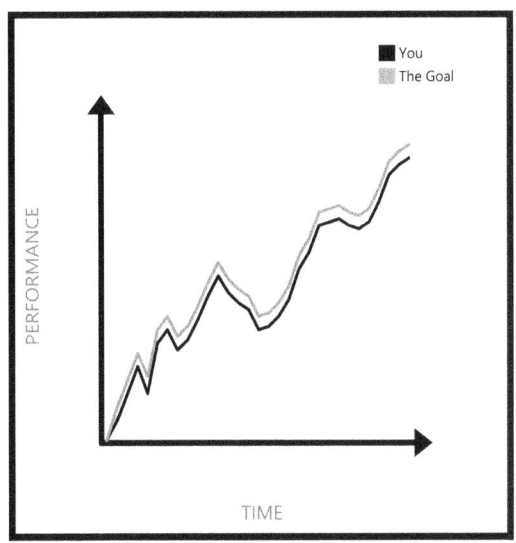

I started climbing in 1995 at a small gym in Cincinnati called Climb Time. With its massive 45° wall, huge volumes, and a heavy focus on bouldering, it was way ahead of its time. I was, of course, initially drawn to the mostly vertical toprope walls. But the destination was clear: the lead wall that started at nearly 45°, quickly went beyond 60°, and then continued damn near horizontal for 30 feet or so. Even though the bolts were close together, floor skimming falls were common.

More important, the way to progress to that lead wall, to those falls, was obvious: bouldering on that giant 45. It was on this wall that I would begin to set my first real climbing goals.

The two managers of the gym, Josh Dees and Chris Eklund, had taken me under their wing and were already nurturing my love of this game. But while I spent most of my time on the topropes, they bouldered. When I eventually worked up the courage to session on this wall, my tutelage kicked into high gear. Chris initially showed me a few basic techniques I hadn't needed to develop on the vertical walls, and then stepped back to let my gymnastic sensibilities take over. Josh would lead sessions with a level of fierce effort that I hadn't previously seen – and still rarely do.

The two were different climbers:

Chris was tall and lean, and deceptively strong. The grace with which he moved overshadowed his finger strength, and I watched him do many of the gym's hardest climbs with what appeared to be ease.

I wanted to do that.

Josh was short and muscular, and attacked climbs with a ferocity and confidence that often saw him through to the finish. He'd invent new beta to fit his stature, contorting himself into extra small boxes or jumping through spaces where taller climbers fit naturally.

I wanted to do that.

I remember a particularly long boulder, going up the left side of the 45, diagonally across to a difficult move on a large blocky volume and continuing down to the lower right corner, only to come back up and over that same volume to finish on top again. Chris flashed it. Josh followed shortly after. A number was being thrown around that I hadn't seen in the gym:

5.13.
I wanted to do that.

I don't remember if I ever finished that hybrid boulder-route at Climb Time. All I can say for sure is that I got sidetracked by crack climbing. I chose a different path, misled by romanticized stories of ethical superiority and boldness. I would follow that path all the way to the second ascent of a 12d called Thurmonuclear Roof Crack, but even then, 5.13 still seemed light-years away.

It wasn't until my complete failure on that 11a, South Central, and watching Yasmeen float it, that I realized just how far astray my chosen path had led. I had a goal but was immediately distracted by the first shiny – or grimy – thing that popped up.

Where exactly had I missed the turn?

5.13. The goal itself. I was chasing a number without knowing the change it would require of me. Without even caring enough to ask what change it would require. Without weighing how the other parts of my life would need to change. Without planning to change at all. I was simply going to keep plodding along doing what I wanted and assume that I was destined for that number because… *because why?*

There was a more important goal right in front of me all along. As I watched Chris and Josh climb, I knew that they were better climbers than me. I didn't need to know the number they were climbing to see that. But I put my focus squarely on that number.

If I had spent a little time wrestling with it and tried to intentionally learn to climb like Chris to reach my goal, and then to learn to climb like Josh to reach my goal, and then went outside to actually try 5.13's, I would have clearly noticed a more accurate goal poking its head around the corner.

I needed to be a better climber.

So how do we measure "better"? How do we know we've reached that goal? Doesn't that just bring us back to the numbers again?

Maybe we don't have to measure it at all. Maybe better is a chase that lasts forever. And maybe partly for the same reasons that I chose an individual pursuit like climbing, and partly due to John's observation of me, I set my ultimate goal in such a way that was open-ended and would put the blame squarely on me if I failed to keep chasing it:

I would become the best climber I could be.

It wasn't about climbing a certain number considered representative of being a better climber. It was about becoming better. And then better. And then better again. Always. If I was in constant pursuit of that, regularly interrogating my methods and resetting my focus, the corresponding numbers would come as stepping stones along the way.

While a goal that lasts forever might sound daunting, there's another important key hidden within my goal that breaks it into easier-to-digest chunks. "I would become the best climber I could be." *Be.* Right now, existing in this moment. I wanted to be the best climber I could be at every moment. Not necessarily in the physical sense – continuous physical improvement isn't realistic, of course. Instead, my goal was to be as good as I could be in any given moment, with no direct comparison to how good I was the day before. To quote Kobe Bryant's Mamba Mentality mantra, "A constant quest to be one's best version of one's self."

This doesn't mean I had to have a singular focus on climbing. Honestly, I couldn't do that even if I wanted to, not then and not now. There are just too many other things that matter to me. My family and learning about and creating various things would always get space. Sometimes climbing would get a lot of space and sometimes it wouldn't. But no matter how much space it had, what I had to do was try to be a little bit better at every moment. If I detoured and was no longer in pursuit, that was on me, and I would have to rectify it on my own.

Now, let's be clear. I didn't come to this conclusion and this goal by simply sitting and puzzling it out. It took a humbling failure and some harsh – but true – words from someone I admired to spur me into recognizing where I actually needed to go. These things laid bare who I had become as a climber and showed me that who I fundamentally was – an amalgamation of my strength and weaknesses, experiences and decisions, emotions and logic – just wasn't enough to get me where I hoped it would. I couldn't just wait for the changes to take place.

I was going to have to constantly pursue that change.

Get Over Yourself

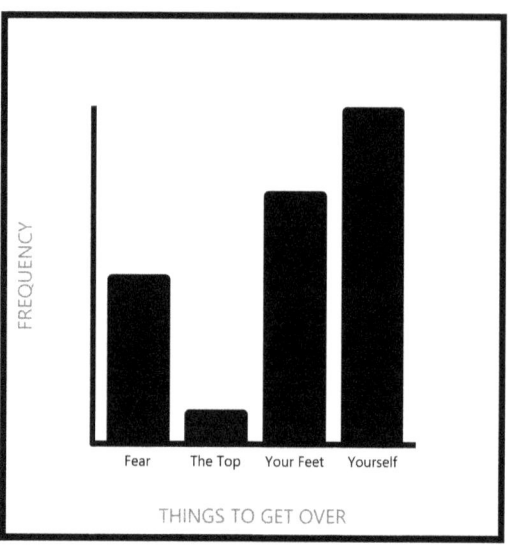

In the early 90s, Colorado legend Skip Guerin completed a sought-after problem on Flagstaff Mountain in Boulder. As it had repelled several climbers before, it required a certain amount of confidence just to attempt, but being a traverse at a popular training area, it invited anyone to try it. He called the problem Over Yourself so that when people were working on it, and of course, failing, he could ask them, "Have you gotten over yourself yet?"

It's possible Skip was just having fun. But to paraphrase the old saying, truth is often spoken in jest. The tongue-in-cheek name had hit on an irrefutable fact of completing challenging goals: You have to get over yourself.

At 32 years old, I decided to return to climbing and dedicate myself to becoming the best climber I could be. This meant I would need to become a regular at the climbing gym again. I knew I needed to ease my way back in, so I traded the steep powerful bouldering of Climb Time for the more approachable lead routes of RockQuest, another local gym. When I signed in that first day, the person at the desk recognized my name.

"I've seen you in the guidebooks!"

It was basically a setup.
I walked into the gym feeling myself, tied into a 5.10 toprope to warm up, got ridiculously pumped, and fell off. I eventually made it to the top, but not before falling on nearly every move of the top 20 feet.
People were watching. Or at least I thought they were.

My next route was easier. A lot easier. And the next, and the next. My immediate goal was to be able to stay on the wall for longer without getting pumped. I figured that if I got myself pumped and learned to climb within that discomfort, pushing it further and further before reaching failure, I'd slowly adapt and eventually be able to do the same at a much higher level of difficulty.
If people were going to watch, I wanted them to see me putting in work. Even if that meant taking a big step backward to find a better way forward.
Sure, some people may see a moment in time and dwell on it. Me falling off of 5.8, so pumped I could barely untie. They wouldn't understand it.
Most, however, will notice the bigger picture. They'll eventually connect the dots between all of the moments in time they've witnessed and what those moments led to.

Before long, I could lap that 5.10 that had spit me off on day one. A couple of months later, I was doing the same on 5.11. Climbing up, down, and back up. Every single session in the gym I was searching for the line between barely hanging on and failure. I would purposely cross the line, fearing I might actually be losing sight of it. I became obsessed with finding ways to push myself over the line on 5.10's and 5.11's. I needed to know every possible failure scenario so that I'd never fall off of that grade again.

Only by intentionally, systematically, and consistently chasing failure did I know exactly what I was currently capable of doing.

And people were *definitely* watching.

They saw me willingly fall off of 5.10 in front of everyone so that I'd eventually be able to climb 5.12 – or even harder. Many people would start doing the same, only to turn back when they couldn't get over themselves. Some stuck with it and embraced the pursuit of failure. More and more, it caught on. A culture of going for it began to take hold in the gym, a place that only a year earlier had been essentially a social gathering spot where people rarely fell off, and even more rarely improved.

Many of those people climbed harder than they ever imagined they would.

Me included.

With no goal, it's easy to let ego guide the way. We want to look good when we do things. We want to appear masterful. The problem is, that implies that we've reached our final form. Having a goal indicates, even to ourselves, that we have something still to strive for. An open-ended goal means we always will, and we'll always be rewarded for being humble in our approach.

For getting over ourselves.

Macro Commitment

In his book, *The Talent Code*, Daniel Coyle writes of a study by Australian music educator Gary McPherson that aimed to figure out why some kids develop skills faster than others when taking music lessons. Starting a few weeks prior to beginning their lessons, 157 randomly chosen children, averaging 7 to 8 years old, were followed all the way through high school graduation.

After the first year of the study, the results were what you would expect: Some kids were crushing, some were floundering, most were somewhere in the middle.

The researchers looked to their massive collection of data to determine what made the difference. None of the factors they expected to play a role mattered. To their surprise, the thing that made the difference was the level of commitment *prior* to the music lessons. The subjects had been split into three groups based on their answer to how long they saw themselves playing this instrument. The kids who imagined themselves doing this for a long time had vastly outperformed the others.

Even with only 20 minutes of practice a week, the long-term committed kids progressed faster than the short-term kids who practiced for 90 minutes.

And when those more committed kids got the same 90 minutes of practice time, they outperformed the short-term-commitment group by 400 percent.

Coyle quotes McPherson as saying, "We instinctively think of each new student as a blank slate, but the ideas they bring to that first lesson are probably far more important than anything a teacher can do, or any amount of practice. It's all about their perception of self."

I was committed for the long term, but with my ego on the line, could I remain committed?

If you've read my first book, *The Hard Truth*, you already know my affinity for the phrase "Throw your hat over the fence." If you haven't, it's a phrase that my grandpa would use anytime I repeatedly said I wanted to do something but hadn't done it yet. Essentially, if you want to climb the fence but can't muster the courage, throw your hat over. Now you've got to climb the damn thing, or the hat is lost forever.

The snapped banana on the cover of that book came to symbolize commitment for many people, some going as far as getting the image tattooed.

I'm not quite that committed.

In a game like climbing, commitment often conjures images of big, scary runouts finishing with an all-points-off dyno. That's not what we're talking about. We're talking about commitment to the bigger picture.

Set a training schedule and follow it.
Set a climbing schedule and follow it.
Let your life partners, climbing partners, and career partners know the importance of these schedules. Make sure they understand.
In the gym, stick to the plan no matter how your ego feels about it.
Outside, stick to the plan no matter how your ego feels about it.
Get on the project when you plan to get on the project unless conditions actually make it impossible.
Have a backup plan for the rare time when conditions actually do make it impossible.
When your performance season is over, plan the next training and performance seasons, and repeat.

That sort of commitment. Macro level commitment. I-plan-to-play-this-instrument-forever level of commitment.

When I came to this realization, my primary responsibility was as a dad to a daughter with whom I spent one day every week and two days every other weekend, something that I wasn't willing to compromise. I was working 50-60 hours a week in a physical job as a mural artist and decorative painter. On average, I went outside to climb six days a month. I was still making music and trying to keep up some semblance of a social life.

So that sort of commitment – I had to get really good at it. Like I said, I based a whole book around it. I threw my hat over the fence. Many times.

It would take a while, but I would come to realize that my ability to commit on this macro level would mask a lack of commitment at a less obvious level.

Eventually, I would have to address it.

Preparation Affords Confidence

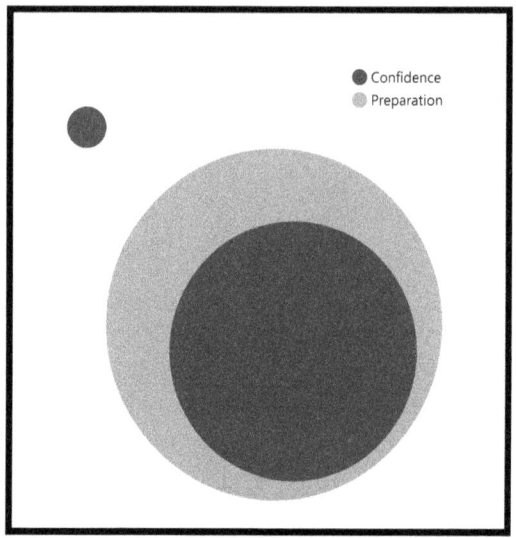

In 2008, an already legendary emcee named Brownsville Ka released his solo debut, *Iron Works*. It caught the attention of GZA, the lyrical genius and elder statesman from the Wu-Tang Clan, who invited Ka to join him in the studio to work on a song for his upcoming solo album, *Pro Tools*.

Over the beat for what became the first song on the album, "Firehouse", Ka spit:

> *My life rest in a .45, aim for head, chest fortified*
> *Sons look for revenge, out of stress, daughters cry*
> *Got to do it here, can't afford to try.*

When he finished, GZA, impressed, asked, "Yo, you got more?"

"I got 20 years more," Ka replied.

He had prepared. For what, he wasn't sure, but he showed up prepared and confident.

Got to do it here, can't afford to try.

On the day I began writing this book, I saw the news that Ka had passed. I went back to this song. In this same verse, just a couple of bars later, he raps:

*Slow and steady win the race,
step aside, let the tortoise by.*

I've been that tortoise. I *am* that tortoise.

I had a goal and I was committed, but I didn't necessarily know what I was doing. I didn't know the best way to prepare. I didn't know about energy systems or metabolic pathways. Hangboarding wasn't popular. There weren't yet training companies and climbing coaches. I didn't know a lot of what I do now.

Frankly, I didn't need to.

Not knowing didn't hold me back from diving headfirst into trying to improve. Back then, there was hardly anybody who *did* know. Eric Hörst had written a few good books about training and Udo Neumann had published *Performance Rock Climbing* with Dale Goddard. There were a handful of good bloggers, most notably the Anderson Brothers and Dave MacLeod.

But I'd also been an athlete. I'd learned that practice or training gave me a certain kind of swagger when walking into a competition. Preparation doesn't need to be exact. It doesn't need to be perfect. The most impactful benefit of preparing for any goal is that it allows you to show up with confidence.

I knew that swagger was important. It might still be the most important.

Got to do it here, can't afford to try.

Train What Matters

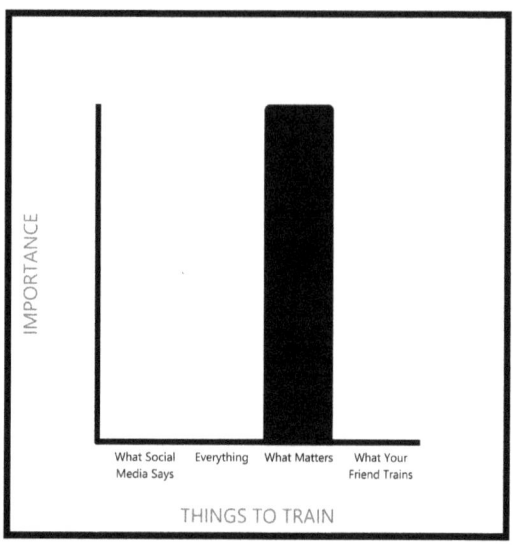

You don't have to train everything all the time.

I'll repeat that:
You don't have to train everything all the time.

It sounds simple, but a quick browse through social media or my email inbox would lead you to believe otherwise. The truth is, we only need to train what we need, particularly in the face of a pending goal.

My major goal was to become the best climber I could be. But it wasn't the immediate goal. Climbing 5.13 would have to happen along the way. But it wasn't the immediate goal, either. First, I needed to be able to hang on for much, much longer.

So that's what I trained.

Laps and laps and hours on the wall. Spending an enormous amount of time completely pumped and learning to exist in that space. Learning to revel in it. To look forward to it.

I knew that Red River Gorge 5.11's and 12's didn't have very many moves that would challenge me. I knew I was a smart enough climber to find my way to do the moves that did. So I barely bouldered. I barely trained any strength or power.

Hours on the wall.

It got to the point where I knew that if there was a jug within the next 10 moves, it was likely I could completely recover and send. And in the Red, on 5.12, there's almost always a jug within 10 moves.

Over my first two seasons spent sport climbing, that single track approach saw me up seventy 5.10's, sixty-five 5.11's, and sixty-two 5.12's including my first 12b onsights.

When I bumped up against a 12c, Wild Gift, that had more difficult moves in a row than I could muster, I changed my training to focus on power endurance. I learned in the gym to keep my movement at a high level even when that deep pump began to set in. I settled down and breathed. I placed my feet carefully even when I felt rushed. I connected more and more hard moves in a row.

A few weeks later, I returned to Wild Gift and did it easily. That same day I went to a different crag, Left Flank, to try a short and powerful 12d that was also notoriously continuous, Stunning the Hog. It took a couple of tries, but when I clipped the chains, I lowered off and repeated it immediately.

A few weeks later, I did my first 13a. *In just five tries.*

I had still never trained finger strength.
Read that again.

Sure, I had played on a hangboard, doing pullups on small holds. But I had never done any dedicated finger strength training. A lack of finger strength just didn't seem to be holding me back. Instead, I was still doing laps on harder and harder terrain.

The next year I managed to send sixty-one 5.12's, including my first 12d onsights, nine 13a's, and my first two 13b's.

When planning the next training cycle, I continued to look for what I needed. It was clear that moves were getting harder at the level I was reaching, so I started spending half of my training time on short, hard boulders.

The next year I sent twenty-four 5.12's, three 13a's, three 13b's, and my first two 13c's. I explored a couple of 13d's and realized that the holds were getting quite a bit worse.

Only then did I add finger strength training into the mix and change my on-the-wall training to bouldering and power endurance on boulders.

This doesn't need to be, and shouldn't be, your timeline or your methods. When there is an imminent goal that you are chasing, you have a choice to make about how to prepare. Your preparation should reflect that goal. However, if you spend more than two minutes on Instagram or YouTube, you'll begin to think that you need to be training everything at all times or you'll wither away and never be a good climber. It just isn't true.

Not everyone needs to lift weights three days every week. Not everyone needs to hangboard all year round. Not everyone needs to always be training endurance or power or anything else.

You only need what you need.

Set intentional goals. Pay attention during the chase. You'll know what you need.

Build Something to Stand On

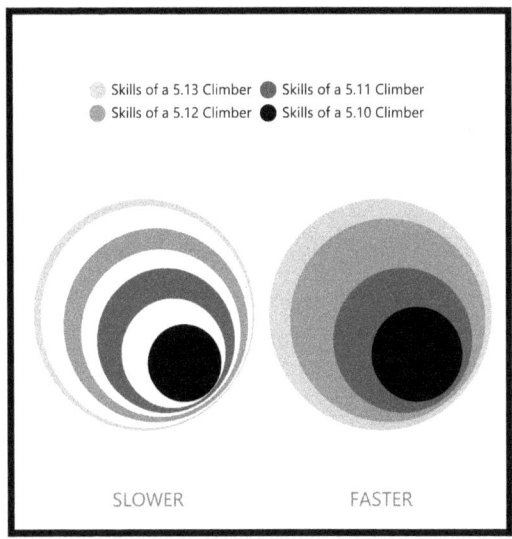

I'm an N-of-1, it's true, but I can point to dozens of cases, maybe hundreds, that clearly dispute the idea that the faster path to harder grades is to just train in the gym and then jump straight to the harder grades. It's entirely possible, probable even, that building a bigger base of easier climbs is actually the faster way to the top grades.

I understand the draw. These numbers that we use to represent the difficulty of a climb also correlate to our ability as a climber. Climbing a harder number should, in theory, mean that we've become a better climber.

The problem is, we all know it doesn't actually work that way.

Goodhart's Law states, "When a measure becomes a target, it ceases to be a good measure."

While Charles Goodhart was an economist, and as far as I know, not a climber, climbing grades are an easy example of this law.

When we use a grade, say 5.13, to represent our own progression or ability, we begin to aim for it. For the climber that takes the approach of building a teetering tower of only a few 5.12's before becoming consumed by a single 5.13, there's a steep opportunity cost. The cost is that they can't spend that time climbing 5.12's, thereby losing out on the valuable experiences those 5.12's offer.

So when they finally achieve that goal of climbing 5.13, it's no longer a measure of how good a climber they are, but simply of how difficult that one rock climb is. For these climbers, it often requires the same multi-season campaign to climb their next of the same grade.

The people who instead aim at climbing on and sending lower grades, gradually building a pyramid – not just of grades but of skills, tactics, experiences, and right and wrong decisions – might still take multiple seasons to arrive at that 5.13 grade. The difference is, that first 5.13 will take fewer attempts, come at a much lower opportunity cost, and lead to their next of the grade happening much faster. That number will be a better representation of their ability. Still a flawed representation, but a better one.

Everyone has their own version of what being a "5.13 climber" – or whatever grade – means. I don't necessarily know what my metric is, but now that I've done a hundred of the grade, in every style, on several types of rock, and in different areas, I'm fairly sure I've reached it. Most of us don't believe that doing one of a grade makes you that level climber. And yet that's the target we often aim for.

To be honest, I didn't build my massive base on purpose. It was incentivized. At the time, the popular website and database redriverclimbing.com had a points system with a public leaderboard that showed accumulated points gained by climbing routes in the Red. Climbing two 11b's got you as many points as climbing a single 13c. And like with any game, I wanted to win. So I climbed a lot of routes. But I also wanted to climb harder.

To make sure that I stayed in the game and didn't get lured into projects too quickly, I came up with a rule for myself. When I onsighted a new grade, I got to spend a day on a project that was three letter grades higher. If I onsighted two of that grade, I got an additional day. Three onsights, and that project level was open.

So I never even considered trying 13a until I had onsighted 12b. In that quest, I tried a lot of 12b's – doing 13 in a season, seven of them second go, before finally onsighting two in the same session. My first 13a required only those two sessions I had opened up – five attempts. I stayed true to my rule and didn't try another 13a until I had onsighted another 12b and opened the grade entirely. That one also took five attempts. A month later, the next required only four tries, and three days after that, I did a 13a the second time I tied in.

Of course, there are only so many routes, and as it gets more sparse in the upper grades or you climb out a local area, this rule becomes harder and harder to follow. But it provided the constraints I needed to build a base that served me well, all the way to 13c.

To be honest, I hesitate to either romanticize or vilify the numbers. They matter because they are the measurement system we have, but what matters more is what we can learn from those lower grades that make up the base. That's where we gain the qualities needed to send the next level grades.

These lower grades are the arena where we're able to learn about getting pumped but holding it together. To learn how it feels when we've stayed long enough at a rest. To keep going when there isn't a rest that's sufficient. That we actually *can* make that big pull off that small edge when we're tired. It's where we'll believe we've got it done just to be spit off at the top, causing us to reevaluate. Where we learn more tactics that we didn't need at 5.11. Doing links or lowpointing or exploring new methods or tweaking beta to be more efficient. Where we're asked to climb above bolts and still try hard on moves we might not complete. To step on footholds that are less than desirable. To clip from stances that we wouldn't have called stances just a year earlier.

Yes, we will encounter all those things at the higher level as well. And we'll likely encounter many of them at once. The problem is that without some of the foundational skills learned at the lower levels, we might never realize the better solutions for this higher-level puzzle.

But if we build that base, we will.

The Art of Execution

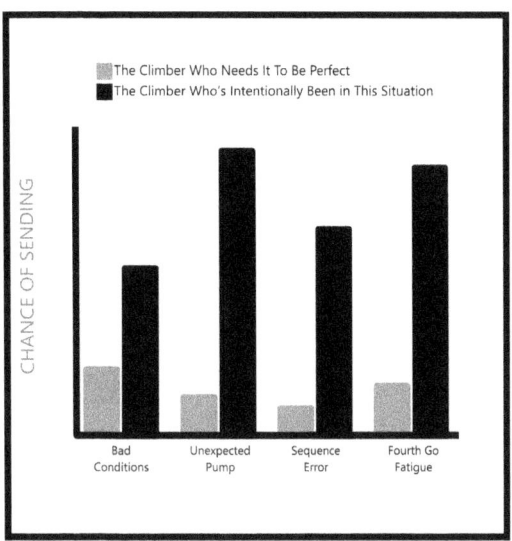

When you start with a big, abstract goal that's open-ended and requires a high level of awareness to even realize that you've gotten to the finish, there's one thing you must do during the chase:

Collect data.

For climbers, sends are that data. Failures are valuable data as well, of course, and there's no doubt we'll be collecting those. However, the positive data that will push us closer to our goal in a more efficient manner is the data associated with clipping the chains. We stack those blocks up to build our base.

Hidden within that data is one skill that is often overlooked:

How to send.

How to actually execute the plan that leads to the desired outcome. All of the strategy and tactics are massively important, but it's the doing of those things that means the most.

Because ultimately, you're going to have to do it. Again and again.

Executing requires more than the academic understanding of what will be more efficient or how to fix the mistakes you made on your previous attempt. Writing all of the moves on paper and obsessively planning out your next go won't do it for you. It won't make the actual task of executing any easier. The only way to practice it is to go for it and risk failure. Repeatedly.

But again, we still need sends to tell us our process worked.

Which is why we practice this skill on easier terrain, where more of our experiments will result in sends. Routes that can be done in a few attempts – if you get it right and give enough effort. Onsight attempts. Two or three session mini projects. If you can get running beta for a challenging flash attempt, it's a fantastic way to see how quickly you can synthesize what you're experiencing with someone else's beta, decide on what's important in the moment, and execute.

At first, the execution will be relatively easy. Not because you're great at it, but because you'll undershoot. You won't yet know what you're capable of. And there are lessons to be had there.

But the real gold will come in that moment when you've gotten the sequence right, you've found the necessary efficiencies, confidence is overflowing, and then with only a few moves left to go before you reach easier terrain and certain success, something unexpected smacks you in the face.

You aren't really pumped. You just can't seem to get on that foot well enough to make that next big pull to the better holds. Then you're overgripping. Then you *are* pumped.

How do you respond?

This is when you learn to execute. Or you don't. The choice is yours.

Until you've found some similar scenario many times over, on terrain where escape from failure is actually possible for you, you'll probably fall off.

You won't yet be able to remind yourself that even though it feels like certain failure right now and that you can't possibly do another move, there are jugs just ahead that you can recover on. You won't yet have the knowledge that you can switch into a grind mode where falling off of 5.11 terrain is damn near impossible. You definitely won't be able to flip that switch at will.

You won't yet have the skills required to realize that you can retreat one move to that slightly incut edge that will give you just enough to shake out that arm for a couple of seconds and collect your thoughts. Just enough to get your heart rate down a few beats. Just enough to push the doubts away.

You won't yet have the skills to reinitiate the sequence and keep this new mindset. To look down at that slopey, slippery foot and press on it with complete confidence even though only a week earlier this was one of those moves that you "had to be fresh for."

These are all skills you need. You can't get them on a hangboard or from a barbell. Ever. You won't get them doing ARCing laps at the gym, no matter how much aerobic endurance you gain. You might be able to find them if you spend all of your time on hard projects, but it will take eons.

I don't have that kind of time.

As a weekend warrior with limited time, I needed to collect those skills as quickly as possible. "Next go for sure," just wasn't an option.

"Next go for sure" sounds pretty damned efficient, but it requires more than you think. That one more attempt may very well require another day. For a weekend warrior that might be an entire week. If, like my schedule back then, every weekend wasn't an option due to other responsibilities, it can mean half a month. And you'll have to talk your partner into going back to that same place. Again. But you already owe them a session elsewhere on their project.

It could be a month before you get back.

Get rid of "next go for sure." Learn to do it now.

Stronger Is the Wrong Answer

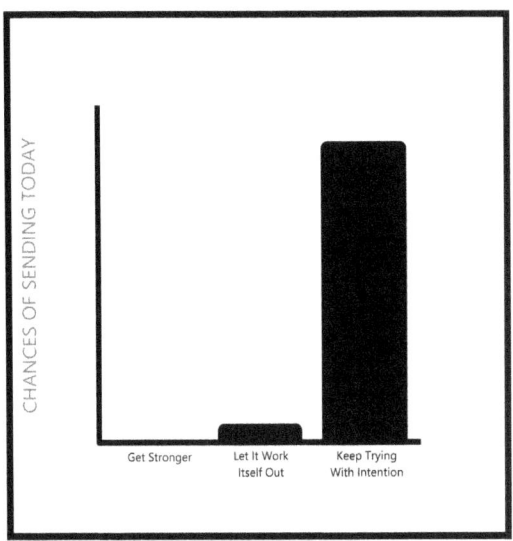

You didn't choose to put time into this rock climb because you thought you weren't strong enough. And you didn't choose to put time into this rock climb to be a passive participant.

However, I often hear the same two refrains from people trying their projects:

> "I think I just need to get stronger."
> "I'll just keep at it. It'll come together."

Getting stronger takes a lot of time. You aren't going to do it with a session in the gym, and it won't happen before next weekend. Waiting for a climb to just "come together" assumes you have no control over the process, which is just, well, sad.

Instead, particularly if you have a time-sensitive goal – and let's be honest, the clock is always ticking – you have to actively seek out the way that you can get it done in the shortest time possible.

Trying it from the ground again with that same beta hoping that something magical happens – and then complaining that you aren't strong enough when you still fall from the same move – is not the way.

Not ever.

Blaming your failure on a quality that will likely take years to develop is simply a convenient place to hide from reality.

We as humans are actually pretty good at not overreaching our abilities. We're also pretty good at underreaching our abilities, but that's another story entirely. Point is, if you chose this climb to put effort into, it's likely because you're capable of it. Because it's possible. And possibility is alluring. It requires us to be just that little bit better.

Which is what we all want. To be a little better.

So stop with the excuses and bad tactics, and choose to get to work at being better.

Conditions Matter, but Not as Much as You Think

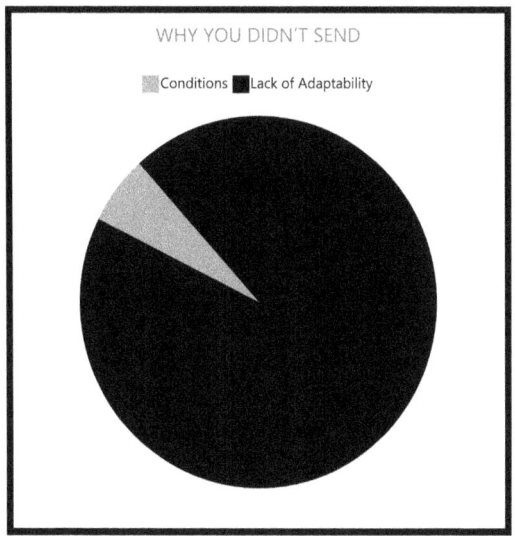

Alex Megos is often cited as an example of how it's possible to climb 5.14 even in horrible conditions. He has openly said, "There is no too short, too tall, too heavy, too warm, too wet, or too humid. There is just one excuse: too weak."

Frankly, this resonates with me. I get it. Team sports were never for me because I want to be the one to blame when things don't go well. I rise to the occasion when I'm to blame. So I appreciate the sentiment.

But Alex Megos is wrong.

In fact, when I spoke with him for my climbing history podcast, *Written In Stone*, he complained about the conditions in the Red and immediately caught himself, realizing his hypocrisy and finally admitting that yes, conditions *do* matter.

We all breathed a sigh of relief because we could put that excuse back in our bag.

Now it's our turn to come clean. We have to admit that we've been overusing that excuse.

Well into my quest to become the best climber I could be, I began taking people under my wing and helping them find their way to be productive climbers. To chase their own goals.

At the time, I was getting closer to my own limits, closing in on 13d and 14a. My responsibilities at work and home were also increasing. So I was choosing to not get sucked into days out in bad conditions, opting instead to stay home and get work done so that I could make it out when good conditions lined up with my days off.

The problem is, the people I was mentoring would do the same.

And when the good conditions arrived, they'd waste them by not being prepared with the skills needed to capitalize on the temps. They hadn't built a base. They hadn't learned to execute.

I had already spent several seasons climbing straight through the humid summers and bitter cold winters in the Red. I'd amassed thousands of routes – many hundreds just a number and a half below my upper limits. I'd learned those skills.

For the majority of the climbing they should have been doing, conditions just didn't matter. Same as they didn't matter for Alex Megos, who had unlimited time to climb and chose to continue building his base on 5.14's that weren't that difficult for him. Seems astonishing to have a base at that grade, but it was his base, nonetheless.

If you have the time and can afford to build your base, the perfect time to stress-test your skills is when conditions aren't great.

Can you find new rest stances when it's humid and slippery and you're over-gripping? Or can you continue moving and realize you didn't actually need that rest? Or can you calm yourself down and relax your grip?

If you're a weekend warrior who has narrow windows in which to wrap up your goals, you can't afford not to use those less-than-ideal days to gain critical skills.

Why would you expect to be able to keep it together on your project during that long, runout 11d exit when you're pumped and fatigued and falling off, if you've only ever tried to climb 11d when everything lined up perfectly?

Or what happens when you get through the crux of your big goal later in the day than you expected and you're in the direct sun facing a slippery granite slab? It's easier climbing, sure, but you never climb in the sun. You're thrown off by the shadows and how greasy everything feels because you refused to go do those easier things when it was warmer than perfect.

Your strategy needs adjusting.

If you want to be prepared to take advantage of the best conditions, it's imperative that you accept how little they actually matter.

Training Principles Don't Apply to Performance

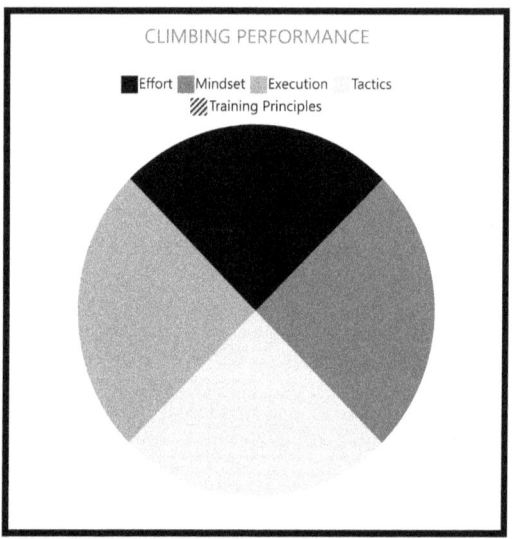

Performance is, by definition, an entirely different monster than training. I would love to assume you already know that, but it's worth saying. Worth it because, for some reason, more and more often I see training principles appearing in the performance environment. Even worse, they are often misunderstood, misinterpreted training principles.

> "I'm not going to try it again because you should only try really hard things when fresh. I'm a little tired, so I'll wait until next week to maximize my skill-adaptation potential."

> "Volume isn't good for building tendon strength, so I'm going to cut it short today. I've done 27 moves, and that's over my threshold already."

"I'm not going to do any climbing during my warmups. I've got a Tension Block, so I'll be able to get my fingers recruited optimally that way, and all of those easier climbs are just 'junk mileage'."

"I gave it my best effort, but based on my single attempt, it's clear the rate of force development in my finger flexors is a shade too slow, so I'll be going back into the gym for a few months before I try this one again."

I've actually heard climbers say these things.

Training is hot right now. The terminology makes you seem smart, even if only to yourself. I mean, self-worth goes a long way, so keep doing it. Particularly nowadays, everyone seems to be training and talking about training. I'm not knocking it – I make my living from it and enjoy it as much as I enjoy climbing. But too much of a good thing is, well... too much.

But here's the thing: when you blur the lines of training and performance, you're inevitably going to slow the growth of your performance. If you can learn to keep your training and your performance separate, then both are far more likely to improve.

There's an old stoic saying that goes, "Only a fool would charge into battle with a dull blade, but a bigger fool would be somebody constantly sharpening his blade and never going to battle."

We have to ask ourselves:
What are we training for?
Are we training just to be able to train harder?
Are we continuing to sharpen our blades at the expense of going into battle?

I hope not. Personally, I'm looking forward to the battles.

In that rare, precious instance when you've gotten all of your work done, the babysitter has shown up, and you've finally found yourself in the performance space, whether that is sport climbing, bouldering, big walls, some greasy Moon Board tucked away in some humid garage, or the new set in the climbing gym…

Stop sharpening the blade and charge into battle. *Try hard.*

All bets should be off. You should be giving every possible effort that you can. Tying in again even as the sun is dropping below the horizon or the passive-aggressive teenage desk employee has turned off the music *and* the lights. Yes, even if your coordination is fatigued and the project is a technical test piece. Nobody ever shouted "A muerte!" during training and meant it. "A muerte!" is for you, right now, trying to get this thing done despite your body failing and everything going against you.

And yes, warming up your fingers using a Tension Block, or Fingers of Fury Baby Boss, or whatever, is a good idea for the sake of recruitment and effort. It makes great sense, particularly for hard, finger intensive training. But if your project is a pumpy cave climb and there's no hold smaller than two pads, is there really a reason to maximize recruitment? Would you maybe be better off getting on a long warmup climb and finding the headspace to try hard and keep your movement together even as the pump begins to creep in?

It might help to try to develop two different mindsets. In training, you're a scientist. Your goal is to utilize theory, research, and experience to optimize learning, building, and progression. But when you are standing in front of the proj, you're an athlete. A performer. LeBron James. Serena Williams. Tom Brady. Sha'Carri Richardson. Michael Phelps. Eliud Kipchoge. You are there to do whatever it takes to succeed. *Right now.*

See, training and practice are rooted in the pursuit of failure. The entire goal is to find that thing that is just that little bit too hard, and to figure out how to systematically improve in a way that can be adapted across a range of situations. Then once sent, to immediately move the goalposts slightly and make it a little harder or more complex so that you're incentivized to keep improving. To keep sharpening the blade.

Performance, on the other hand, is the pursuit of success. The goal is to send. Sure, maybe just barely, but to send regardless. During performance, you can throw out the training rules. It doesn't have to be done well or done efficiently, just done. Keep your training principles – especially the misunderstood, taken-out-of-context principles that lack nuance – out of performance.

Mid-battle is not the time to worry about sharpening your blade.

The Key

"You have the key, right?" she asked.
"What key?" I asked, surprised at her choice of words.

How did she know? Did she know?

Rewind a couple of weeks, and I'm lowering off of Ultraperm, 13d, having fallen off the final hard move for the fifth time in a row, and third time that day. Normally I wouldn't be frustrated so quickly, but my first push toward 13d the season prior had ended much the same, falling off the last hard move many, many times.

I untied, sure I was finished for the day, and dug into my pack in search of whatever food I had left. I sat down and checked my phone that I'd heard buzzing earlier. Five missed calls and eight text messages? Everyone worth talking to knows where I am and that I'm not going to answer the phone. My grandmother, my brother, and my girlfriend had called.

Not a good sign.

All the texts were the same, "Please call us," with the exception of the last:

"Kris, Papaw passed away. We need you here."

My grandfather had been one of the few constants in my life, and from the time I was 10 years old, the closest thing I had to a father. His health had deteriorated over the past few years, but he hung in there, always quick with a joke and toothy grin. I'd been driving across the city a few days a week to pick him up and take him to dialysis. That time in the car together and sitting across from him at the dialysis center was the most time we'd spent really talking, just the two of us, in a long time.

He was there for me as my life fell apart at 16, silently picking up the pieces and storing them away for when I would someday need them. Always quiet and patient, he taught me mostly by example. Advice was never really offered, rather he let me take my lumps and learn my lessons, only offering a net as I was just about to hit bottom. He'd be there every time I fell, never wavering in his support. I eventually pulled it together and reassembled those pieces, even adding a few new ones: a daughter and a girlfriend that he never ceased to dote on.

The days following his death were a whirlwind of activity searching for documents and helping with whatever needed to be done around the house. Needless to say, climbing and training took a distant back seat. Sorting through and cleaning out the various sheds and outbuildings, we collected over 50 bags of trash, nearly 30 old tires, and too many ancient pieces of furniture to mention. Something about a family member passing causes neighbors to deliver fried chicken to your door, and with so much work to do, opening a soda became easier than getting ice water. Six days of that routine left my body languid and drained of spirit.

My next trip to the Red was, like so many others that spring, soggy and dreary. Where I was once able to motivate through the gloom, I now succumbed to it. An attempt on Ultraperm ended far below my previous highpoint, and worse yet, just never felt right. No confidence, no motivation, no desire. I didn't care anymore. I didn't want it. What I wanted was to not have to try so damned hard.

Back home, I retreated to my grandfather's work shed, where I had spent so many days as a boy in awe of the tools and know-how that Papaw had. The shed had become a catch-all over the years, but we had stripped away the bulk of the junk. I got down to the business of sorting through memories.

Beneath a pile of ancient tools I found a tiny skeleton key. I'm not sure I'd ever seen it before. Of all the hundreds of things I'd come across in the last week, most of which I had no idea existed, this little key held a certain simplicity. I didn't wonder what it was for, or where it came from. I just wanted to keep it. That night I attached it to my harness, so that I could carry it with me when I was at my best, at my most focused. I told no one.

Packing for the Red a few days later, my girlfriend asked what my plans were, and if Ultraperm was in them.

"I'm not so sure," I answered, "I've basically let it go. It'll be there next season, and I'll come back stronger. I'm just not sure that I can do it right now."

"You have the key, right?"

"What key?" I asked, thinking that she must have seen me tying the skeleton key to my gear loop.

"The key to the route. You know what you need to do. Do it."

Motivation had somehow returned as I laced up under Ultraperm. My neck was so stiff from working on ceiling murals that I couldn't see my own knot and had to have my partners check it, but that hardly mattered. I stood at the stance below the unrelenting steep pockets and focused. I reached back and touched the key, remembered those lessons in patience that I had been given, and began climbing.

The pain of the past few weeks disappeared. There was no struggle. I got to that move with plenty in the tank, and where previously I had thought, *Here's where I fall*, there was no concern at all. I thought of Papaw and how he'd argue with me that he could cut the grass or shovel the snow himself when it was clear that he couldn't. He never even considered that he couldn't do something. I thought of how brave Mamaw was through all of this. I thought of how strong my daughter had been when I told her Papaw was gone.

And I easily did the move.

I had the key.

GROW

2012
Thirteen 5.13's

May, 2012
First 13a flash

November, 2012
Finished longest project ever, Swingline, 13d

2013
Nine 5.13's

Early 2014
Built first training space, The Engine Room

2014
Five 5.13's

October, 2014
First 14a

2015
Turned Power Company Climbing into a full time career

April, 2015
Shoulder surgery

2016
Seven 5.13's

January, 2016
First V10

September, 2016
Moved away from Cincinnati and went on first extended road trip

2017
*Two 5.13's
Mostly bouldering*

April, 2017
Bought a house in Lander, WY

December, 2017
Built home gym, The Machine Shop

2018
*Two 5.13's
Still mostly bouldering*

Pressure on Purpose

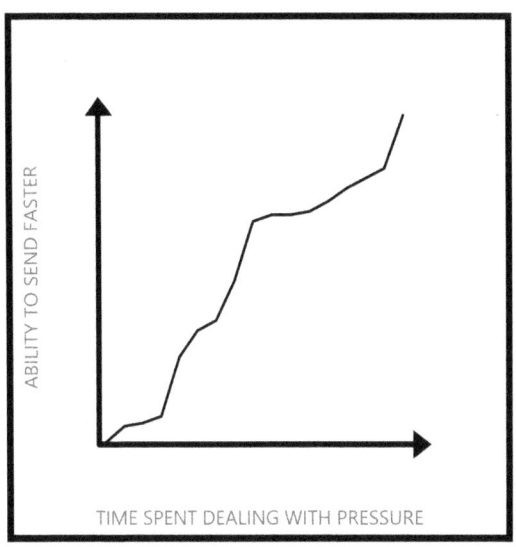

In 2011 while planning a trip to Wild Iris, outside of Lander, Wyoming, I realized that even though I had done some seemingly hard-for-me routes on trips, I had done them relatively quickly. My calibration hadn't quite caught up with my abilities, so these things that seemed like big numbers weren't actually that difficult for me. I wanted to know what would happen if I went all in on something hard on a trip.

Most often, I see climbing trips go one of two ways:

The climber wants to make the most of their time, so they plan to do a high volume of relatively easy routes or boulders.
Or...
The climber has a project in mind that they want to do but within the first few tries they've bailed, opting instead to do a high volume of relatively easy routes or boulders.

We've already established that up to a point, doing a large volume of climbing is a good thing. There's certainly nothing wrong with learning about the style of an area by doing a lot of the climbing it has to offer. Neither of these two choices is wrong.

But what I want you to ask yourself is:

Why did you make this choice?

Is it because you don't want to go home "empty-handed"? Is it because you're avoiding the pressure of having to get something done in a certain amount of time?

If there's even an inkling of this, I think I can convince you that on some trip soon you should go all in on one hard route, send or not. Frankly, it might be the best possible thing for your climbing.

For most climbers, the at-home projecting process is comfortable. There's plenty of time to work out the micro beta and all of the subtleties. There's time to rethink and rework the beta. Time to wait for better conditions and time to have side quests. If you don't get it done this season, you can do it next season. There's no pressure.

But pressure is a valuable constraint. Leaning into pressure that is manageable, but not easily so, can force you to focus on what's necessary. Your process will get more efficient. Pressure also adds a layer of meaning to a timeframe. You'll care more about each attempt, and you'll learn the impact that caring can have on your climbing. As time winds down and the pressure builds, you'll learn to give everything you have.

If you're lucky enough to have one of those last-possible-attempt-of-the-trip sends, then you'll be far better prepared for when a season at home is closing down or weather is moving in. Even when you fall just short, you're learning valuable lessons about dealing with failure.

Up to this point, the pressure I had to perform under had been as a weekend warrior who could nearly always go back and try again. But learning to send faster seemed appealing. I had done my first 13d, a steep power endurance route called Ultraperm, only a couple of months earlier, so why not try to do 13c while in Lander? I'd never done one on a trip before, but two weeks didn't seem like long enough.

That was the point.

The 13c I chose, Atomic Stetson, was one I had tried briefly the previous summer. It had all but shut me down on that trip, but I had spent enough time on it to know it well. I set a replica and trained specifically for it.
Despite all my preparation, first day back on the route I tweaked a finger and couldn't pull on the crux monos at all.
I would have to pivot, but not to something easier. Because I'd thrown my hat over the fence, I wouldn't let the specter of pressure cause me to buckle.

The day prior I'd gone with local strongman BJ Tilden to a new crag, the Sweat Lodge. After onsighting a 12c, I decided to go up a 13c called Ghost Dance, thinking I would check it out for a future time.
Turns out, that time was now. With no tweaky holds, Ghost Dance would have to do. I didn't have time to shop around.

By this time I had done four 13c's, and my first week of steady progress on Ghost Dance seemed similar to the timelines of those routes. However, all of those were sent on my schedule as a weekend warrior rather than on a two-week trip. Rest days and skin care became increasingly complicated. I was running out of both, but couldn't afford to run out of either.

The pressure was building.

With only three climbing days left on the trip, I finally broke through the steep pocketed crux and made the powerful exit moves onto the overhanging prow. It was the end of the day and I was surprised to find myself only one well-rehearsed move from a good rest. I fell off of that move.

The pressure was building.

My wife likes to tell people that when she lowers me off a near-send, after just snatching defeat from the jaws of victory, at which point she would be wrought with frustration, the smile on my face is impossible to erase. One of my favorite things is to be proven wrong by a rock climb. Every time a move unexpectedly spits me off, or a section is harder to link than I figured, it's an invitation to learn something.

But now, what to do? Rest one day and come back with two days available, just in case, but risk being under-recovered? Or rest two days and only have one day to finish it?

I chose to rest two days and then give it everything I had.

The pressure was building.

On my first go of the day, I again punched through the steep pockets. I landed the left-hand throw to the good hold on the little arête, and for the first time, the crease at the base of my middle finger landed on a small, sharp spike, puncturing it in such a way that I couldn't open or close my hand. I felt like I had plenty to make the next big lateral move, but I was stuck. I dropped off, blood dripping from my finger.

The pressure was building.

Next go I was a little more tired, but still made it to that move. *This is it,* I thought. I threw to the good hold on the arête. Same spike. Same inability to close my hand. It ripped through the tape and cut even deeper into my finger.

Pressure.

I mustered all I could for one more go. Same spike. Three times in a row. I knew it was over.

I was proud of the effort I'd put in, even though it hadn't been enough to send. I was going to walk away happy. After all, we were having dinner that night at Amy Skinner's nearby cabin with her and Paul Piana. I'd never had the chance to sit and chat with Paul, and was looking forward to that as much as any of the climbing on the trip.

I packed my bag. As I picked it up to begin the hike out, my wife (then-girlfriend) put her pack down.

"You should try again."

"Are you crazy? There's no way I can do that again."

"But you should try. There's still enough light. You don't just give up. We're here now. One more try, then we'll go to the cabin for dinner with Paul."

I started to argue, but I knew she was right. I had to try again. Either way, it would be a better story to tell Paul.

I unpacked, tied in, and took a deep breath, exhaling sharply.

Same spike. Again. This time, I pulled anyway.

My hand wasn't closed – and it may have only stayed on because of that spike – but I pulled. I stuck the sidepull, walked my feet through, and was on the jug. In the fading light, the heady slab exit was a non-issue. I don't even really remember it.

I was already floating.

A Good Partner Is a Great Asset

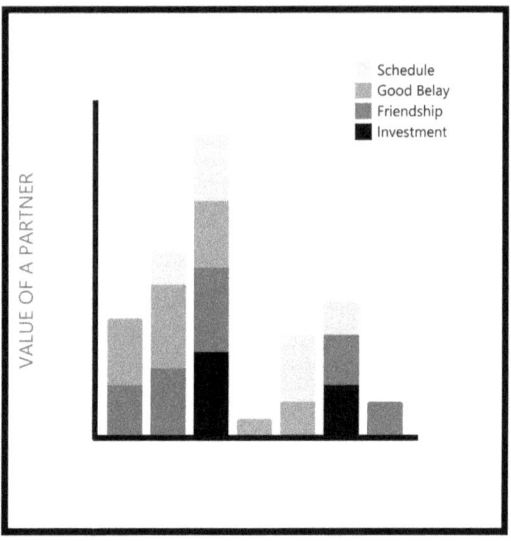

The GMC Wall at the Motherlode is often overshadowed by one of the sections of cliff that made the Red River Gorge world-famous as a climbing destination: the Madness Cave. And while the allure of the Madness Cave is warranted, the climbing itself is fairly simple, particularly when compared to the routes on the neighboring GMC.

Starting off of a high pedestal, in plain view of nearly everyone at the crag, is one of the most classic of the routes in the entire area: Snooker.

I was belaying my friend Taylor Frohmiller on an early morning redpoint attempt in late March. He had put it together quickly, this being only his third time on the route. He started up, having no trouble with the initial boulder or the power endurance crimp section, and soon found himself at the big rest below a little roof and a pumpy headwall. I expected him to make it here without much trouble.

However, I knew Taylor had a bad habit of taking and hanging on the rope when he was feeling like he might not make it. I remembered from doing the route years earlier that the headwall was a little harder than I wished it were, and anticipated that he might try to resort to this bad habit when the pump started to set in.

He didn't spend much time at the rest – certainly less than I'd expected – before launching off, out of my sight, for the several bolt run to the chains. He was moving fast, and pretty soon did exactly what I expected.

"Take!"

I wasn't having it.

"Fuck no!" The whole crag turned to watch. "You *do not* let go! Keep climbing!"

And so he did. Thirty seconds later he shouted down, "But now I'm way above the anchors!"

He trusted me. Maybe a little *too* much.

That was Taylor's first 13a of a breakout year for him, climbing a total of seventeen 5.13's, including his first two 13c's. It was basically the last season that I was climbing harder than him.

And that's exactly what I wanted. Sure, I was acting as coach and mentor, but more than that, we were partners. Great partners.

It didn't necessarily start that way. Taylor was one of the strong kids at the gym who needed some outdoor guidance. Somewhere along the way he had made the great choice to start dating Sarah Rottenberger, and they came as a package deal. That turned out to be great for me, because Sarah was by far the more focused and responsible of the pair.

We would organize our seasons by cross-referencing each other's project lists, planning our training days, and making sure our work schedules didn't interfere with our Tuesday sessions at the Red. They were 21 and 23 years old, but somehow agreed to leave Cincinnati at 5:30 am every week.

Taylor would usually sleep both ways, while Sarah and I talked about life or had George Strait and Prince sing-alongs.

At the crag, we were a well-oiled machine. First there, last to leave, and no down time. We got shit done. A lot of it.

Because we *cared*.

We all cared how each other climbed. I was as invested in their climbing as they were in each other's and mine. Nobody batted an eye about giving up a day they had planned to spend checking out something new or working out beta in order to go belay someone on a redpoint attempt. If there was any debate, it was because none of us wanted to miss witnessing the sends.

A good partner isn't just someone whose schedule lines up with yours. It's not someone you can just trade belays with. Yes, that will absolutely work for a time, but it will never provide the benefits you get from a truly good partner.
There's conversation. There's caring. There's investment. There's energy. There's friendship. There's trust.

Without that, partnership just isn't the same.

A good partner is a great asset, and you need to be a great asset back. I've been lucky to have some great partners and lucky to have times that helped me realize how great they were. I don't really engage in nostalgia, but if I did it wouldn't be for younger days feeling strong and sending.

It would be for those great partnerships.

Shoot Smarter

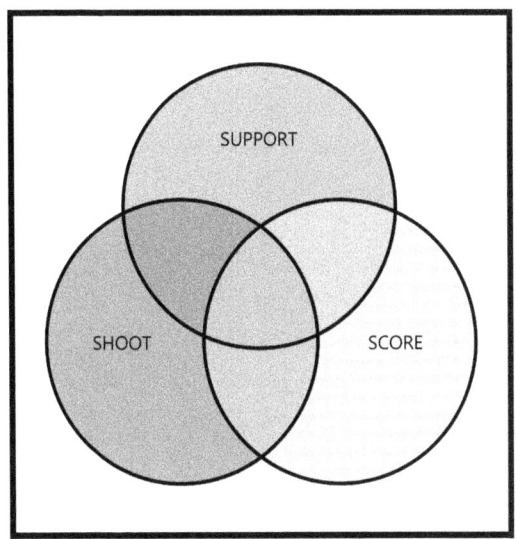

Hockey great Wayne Gretzky is often quoted as saying,

"You miss 100% of the shots you don't take."

According to "The Great One" himself, this was in response to people telling him, since he was 12 years old, that he should shoot more often. He said it in a "yeah, yeah, I know," eye-rolling sort of way, because he believed that it didn't matter who scored, as long as someone scored. But the quote stuck and became one of the most often cited in sports cliché history.

And Gretzky was right, on several counts.

His illustrious 20-year career ended with the most goals scored in NHL history. He wouldn't have scored those goals if he hadn't taken the shots. It also ended with the most assists in NHL history. In fact, he's still over 700 assists in the lead.

He took the shots, yes, but he also knew when to *not* take the shot, and instead feed the puck to an open teammate. He took the *smart* shots.

Only 31 goals behind Gretzky in the record books is Alex Ovechkin. This is an impressive feat, and Ovechkin will likely take the lead at some point soon, but if we look deeper, we see that Ovechkin is 1,257 assists short of Gretzky, and he's taken nearly 1,600 more shots. He's taken more shots on goal than any player in NHL history. Gretzky is 8th on that list. Ovechkin isn't even in the top 50 for assists.

Ovechkin's shots aren't as smart as Gretzky's, and he's not looking for his teammates as often.

If these two were climbers, I'd be calling dibs on Gretzky as a partner.

Much like the redriverclimbing.com leaderboard that influenced my early sport climbing, the NHL has a points system for their players that is separate from the team score. Goals and assists are added together to calculate a representation of how much a player contributes offensively. On this career points list, Ovechkin is 13th all time. Not bad. But at the top, ahead by 400%, is Gretzky.

Imagine if climbers got points for not only their sends, but also for great support. Where would you rank? How about your partners?

There's nothing saying you can't get on climbs that are way over your head and take your shot. It can be a great way to see how your skills and abilities stack up to the next level. You might be capable of more than you expected, or you might grossly overshoot. Either is valuable to know. But we need to be honest about how the shots we choose to take can impact our climbing.

Are you taking shots that inspire you? Or that frustrate and demotivate you? Is it starting to negatively affect your partners? Is it beneficial or detrimental to your climbing? Is it costing you opportunities to try other climbs that might help you progress faster? Are you scoring when you shoot?

And maybe most important, are you trading belays or are you trading assists?

Sure, you can't score if you don't shoot. But if you shoot simply because you're chasing some number, instead of shooting smart, you're going to miss a lot of shots. Give yourself chances, but be discerning.

Be smart. Be Gretzky.

Are You the Same You?

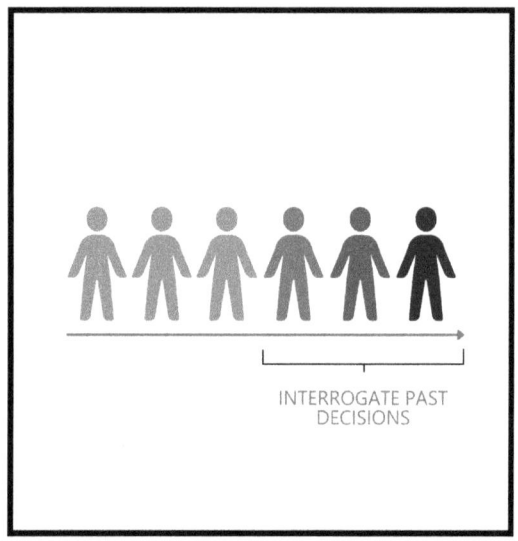

I was working on what would turn out to be my longest-ever project, Swingline, a 13d at a steep, pocketed crag called The Darkside in the Red River Gorge. I had spent parts of several seasons on it, never at the full expense of climbing other things, but it had certainly taken up a lot of my time outside.

I was at the point that I could climb five times in a single session to the final hard move before falling, but I couldn't break through. I had done all of the obvious links. The only thing left to do was send. It just wasn't happening.

I'm a creature of habit. I love routine – to a fault. I had learned that I needed to constantly reevaluate in order to be sure my routine was still serving me and moving me toward my goals. So I would often ask myself an important question:

Are you the same you?

This reevaluation done at work had resulted in a different schedule: four 10-hour days instead of five 8-hour days. This opened up an extra day that I could climb, provided I had partners willing to make the five-hour round-trip haul every week. Thankfully, Taylor and Sarah were always game, even rearranging their work schedules in order to make it happen. This meant my average number of outdoor climbing days per month went from six to 10. I was sending more and improving faster.

But Swingline just wouldn't relent.

Are you the same you?

I wasn't. I was stronger than before. I was better than before. I had let go of the idea that this would be my first 13d and had already completed another. But that wasn't enough.

I also was no longer current with this route. It had been a couple of seasons since I had lowpointed from below the first obvious rest. Since then, I had taken off most of a fall season to remodel a tiny house next door to my grandmother's so that I could help take care of her. I had spent time on other routes. I couldn't just waltz up to The Darkside and expect to be able to pick back up right where I'd left off. I had to rebuild some parts of this relationship.

Over the course of a couple of sessions I moved my current lowpoint down to just below that obvious rest, but only barely scraped through. I realized how hard the crux felt. It had been a long time since I explored beta there, believing I had found my way. So I asked again:

Are you the same you?

I remembered watching a friend send the route in just a handful of tries a year or so earlier. He had used beta for the crux that I had quickly rejected, believing I was too short to replicate it. But while reevaluating, I figured it was worth another try. With the better strength and tension I had built in the gym, I was able to do the crux first try. It felt two V grades easier than the method I'd settled on. I sent next try.

I was definitely *not* the same me.

If I had to characterize my sport climbing up to about 13c, I'd use one word: sloth. I could rest my way up just about anything, and while I *could* climb dynamically, I much preferred to be locked in at all times.

While spending a lot of time at the Motherlode over the years, I'd walked past a route called Take That, Katie Brown hundreds, if not thousands, of times. I hadn't given it much serious consideration; its reputation was that you had to either be tall or really good at climbing explosively. That's where the name comes from, actually. Katie Brown, at 5 feet tall and with a very controlled style, had onsighted pretty much everything at the cliff up to 13d. Hugh Loeffler, at 6-foot-something with long arms, had found a route that required nearly all of his length to connect together. With tongue-in-cheek and Katie's permission, he named the route. I thought it looked incredible, but way out of reach, no pun intended.

But I was no longer that same sloth-like me.

I'd been bouldering, putting a focus on learning to use momentum more effectively, and found that I'm actually pretty good at climbing dynamically. In the late winter after doing Swingline, I was ready to test my new self. Take That, Katie Brown seemed like it might be a good final exam.

I had worked out the moves and started making links, but soon the top half of the route was getting wet from snow melt and runoff. I'd purposely come on freezing days, hoping there would be no melt, but then I'd numb out before I got anywhere near the crux. The wetness continued through the start of spring, and I'd all but given up on getting the route done that season.

One morning at a crag called Drive By, where Taylor and Sarah had projects, we ran into our friend Lee Smith. He was there warming up for his project at a nearby crag, Bob Marley. For the past month, Lee and I had been commiserating about our projects being wet, but on that day, Lee's was dry.

"If mine is dry, yours is dry," he said, suggesting that I should rethink my day.

I looked at Taylor. "How would you feel about a quick pivot to the Motherlode, before it gets too warm?"

He was already packing.

Leaving Sarah to try her project while conditions were good, Taylor and I drove to the Motherlode and hiked straight to Take That, Katie Brown. Lee was right; the route was dry.

On my first attempt, I highpointed, falling near the end of the difficulties. I gave Taylor the option to go back to Drive By for his project.

"You should just do this thing," he said, without hesitation. And so I did.

I *was* a new me. Harder things were within reach. Pun intended.

My first book, *The Hard Truth*, is bookended by essays about my experience climbing Transworld Depravity, my first 14a. On the final cool day of a spring season, I battled through 50 feet of dripping wet 13a exit climbing only to fall at the final move to the clipping jug. For months, I wasn't sure I would go back.

But I was trying to climb 14a by my 40th birthday. After a summer of dedicated training, I decided to go back and finish the job. On the first cool days of the fall, I reacquainted myself with the route, expecting a quick send. A couple of days in, and I had yet to comfortably repeat the hardest crux move. I could do it, making the big lateral move off of a small right-hand edge out to a juggy sidepull, but my feet would cut every time, requiring energy I knew I wouldn't have on a redpoint.

I didn't understand. I thought I was doing the move exactly as I always had, and that as a stronger climber, it should feel easier. But it didn't.

My 40th birthday came and went, and I just couldn't make it through that move. As I slumped on the rope after another unsuccessful attempt, I asked myself a question:

Are you the same you?

No. I absolutely was not. I had spent much of the summer training in our new space, The Engine Room, with that particular edge in mind, knowing that my ability to hold it would make all the difference. I could hang that edge one-handed now. Maybe I had overemphasized it at the expense of good tension? No, I wasn't seeing anything similar on any other moves. My ability to use tension was fine, if not even better than before.

Then, hanging there, I realized that I was giving just as much effort to that move as I always had. But I didn't *need* to. I was essentially – after climbing the 12c intro into the first V8 crux into the short, steep 13a section – doing a one-arm pull up on this edge and pulling my feet off of the holds. I tried again, more relaxed, purposely letting my weight come down onto my feet, and they stayed put.

The following Sunday, I clipped the chains, only 3 weeks late.

Aphorisms and Absolutes

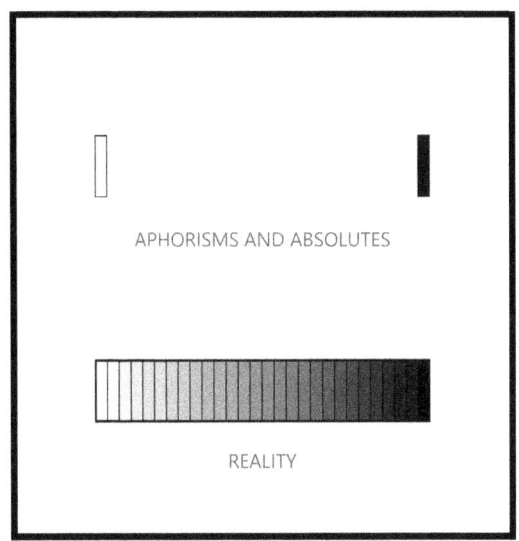

In 2021, Facebook revealed that, according to their data, the average attention span for a video is two seconds.

Two seconds.

Actually, it's 2.4 seconds on desktop, 1.7 seconds on mobile. I suspect if more of our desktops had touch screens that allowed scrolling and swiping, that time of 2.4 seconds would drop.

At the same time, social media is being used as a primary source of teaching and learning for many of us. Climbers are following their favorite coaches and athletes, hoping for that next groundbreaking piece of knowledge. Coaches are turning to Instagram in an attempt to disseminate said knowledge, which is all too often knowledge they came across earlier that week from a different internet climbing coach. Who saw it on Instagram. Or Tiktok. Or Facebook. In two seconds.

So it's not surprising that we end up with black and white information.

> *This* is the way.
> *This* is not the way.
> Do *this*.
> Never do *this*.
> There are *no* exceptions.

Except there are. Always. That's never the only way. Sometimes we do this. Sometimes we do that. Honestly, sometimes we seemingly get better results from doing nothing at all.

If I put my business owner hat on, I get it. It's an attention economy, and with two seconds to catch people's attention, posts need to make a quick statement. Advice has to be strong. Bold. Nuance is… well, nuanced. It doesn't stand up front and center and suck all the air out of the room. Nuance is not attention-grabbing. It's not easy to convey in big bold fonts. Nuance is the gray area. That's where I live. And whether or not you like it, that's where you live too.

I know you might like the black-or-white zone. It seems so simple. So pure. So exact. It gets more views. More likes. More shares. It claims to get predictable results.

> Do *this* and you shall achieve *this*.

I wish.
But it just doesn't work that way.
Instead, there are complex interactions at play. Your diet is different. Your mindset is different. Your height, weight, ape index, experience, metabolism, style preferences, preferred grip types, comfort level on various rock types, risk management skills, available time, available equipment, family obligations, work responsibilities, and so many other things are all different.

The crimp training that you heard is *the* way didn't work for you, so you must be broken. But you were already a crimp master, and your trip was to Horse Pens, where there are a total of two crimps, so of course it didn't improve your climbing. That advice wasn't *for* you.

Pretty much the only absolute statement about training that can be true is that there are no absolute statements about training that can be true.

I'm guilty too. I like provoking. I want you to think. To reconsider.

On social media or in the title of an essay, I might punch you in the face with a statement. I am a business owner after all, and I have to play the game to some degree. But I do my best to follow it with nuance. To let you know that it may not apply to you. And that it might. Especially if it hurt your feelings to begin with.

But if you got excited because my statement validated you, then now – right now – is the time to ignore it. It wasn't for you.

In fact, you should rethink this essay. Am I talking to you? Is there an assumption you need to question? Or are you firmly secure in your gray-area existence?

Do this for every single piece of advice you encounter. Particularly the social media posts with charts and drawings and citations that make a statement of unequivocal truth. They are doing their best impression of black and white.

You and I – and our climbing – exist in the gray area.

Consistency Is Complicated

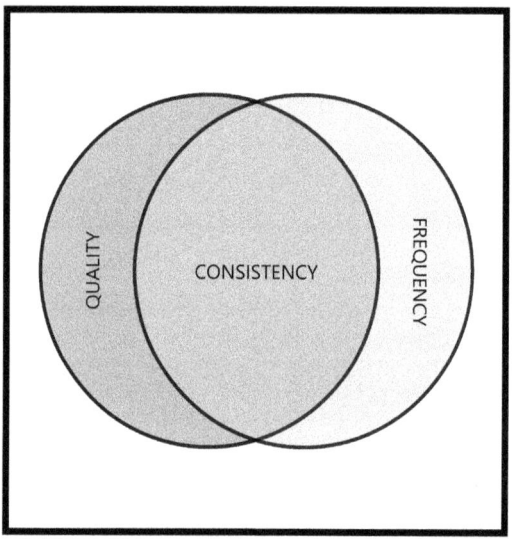

Among those aphorisms bombarding your social feeds is undoubtedly this one:

"Consistency is king."

I mostly, kind of, sort of agree. You probably do as well. But did you make the mistake that so many people make, time and time again? Instead of reading "consistency is king", did you read something different entirely?

"Frequency is king."

This, I strongly disagree with.

Not that frequency is bad. It can be a great thing, but frequency doesn't carry with it the same connotations and subtleties as consistency. And let's be clear – the term consistency is still lacking some nuance that would make it "king", but we'll get to that.

From the *Oxford English Dictionary*:

> **fre·quen·cy** /ˈfrēkwənsē/ *noun*
> 1. the rate at which something occurs or is repeated over a particular period of time or in a given sample.

Many coaches and trainers will follow their "consistency is king" statement with some sort of "you have to show up" messaging. As if somehow, just appearing at the gym will help you improve. I'm sure I've been one of those coaches.

But I don't believe it. You can't just show up. If you are just showing up, you may as well not show up. There needs to be intention. Not every session needs to be – or will ever be – great, but the quality of intention needs to be there.

And that's where we go wrong. Consistency is a function of quality, not just of frequency. You can show up regularly but lack quality. You can have high-quality sessions, but not show up enough. Neither of these are the way.

As usual, the answer lies somewhere in the middle. Showing up often enough to make a difference, with an intention to move the needle in a specific way.

One of my favorite Hip Hop writers, Dan Charnas, wrote a book called *Work Clean* that profiles high-level chefs and breaks down how they organize their work and lives. Chefs are an interesting study because they have to show up, but they also have to produce quality – all on a ticking clock. His definition of excellence resonated with me.

> "If perfectionism is the pursuit of quality at the expense of delivery, then settling for less is the quest for delivery at the expense of quality. Excellence itself is a compromise between the two: quality delivered."

Waiting for the optimal conditions in order to have the optimal session is perfectionism. That's not what we're after. Not in training or performance. We miss opportunities to send and we miss opportunities to learn. We miss opportunities to adapt.

Just showing up whenever it's scheduled simply because you're supposed to is settling for less. That's not what we're after either. A day at the gym or crag with no intention or when we know it's going to go poorly isn't just a lost day – it's a missed opportunity to be productive elsewhere, which could open up future time for a session with more intention.

We should be aiming for what Dan describes as excellence: "quality delivered."

But I get it. It's an aphorism. It's meant to strip away the nuance in favor of an alliterative platitude that's easy to say and easy to remember. Something that will catch the attention of people looking for a magic solution to their perceived problem of not getting good enough fast enough.

And as much as I don't want to admit it…

> "As frequent as possible without sacrificing a high-level of quality is king."

…just doesn't have the same ring to it.

Less Isn't More

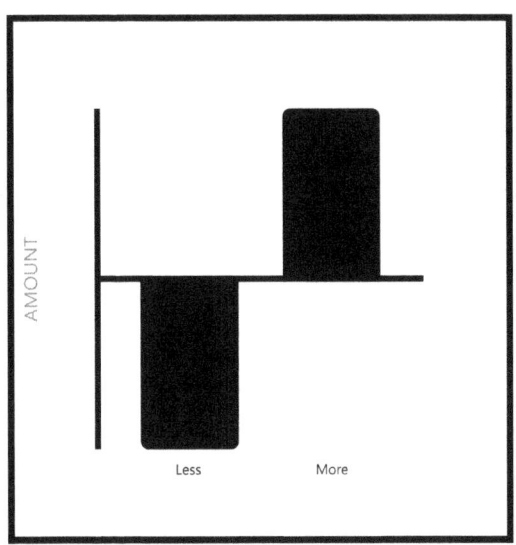

Less isn't more.

It's less.
Sometimes less is *better*, but it's never more. Ever.

Don't fall for it.

That's it. That's the lesson.

Science Isn't Right

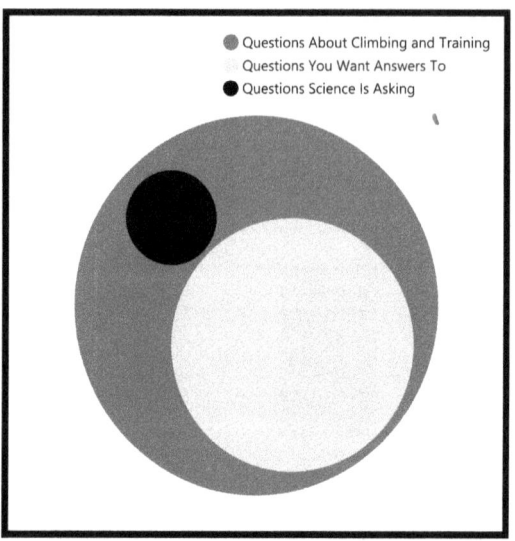

Science isn't right. It isn't wrong either. It's just not trying to directly answer the questions we're asking.

Since the beginning of my exploration of learning and improvement, I've had a fraught relationship with science. At that time there was very little research on climbing, and what was out there wasn't very applicable. So I looked to other sports. Running had been looked at extensively, and I could easily equate sprinting with bouldering, longer distances with massive endurance pitches, and middle distances or long sprints with the average sport climb. Not a perfect equivalent – not even remotely close actually – but it seemed close enough.

At first, I latched on to larger principles within the papers – overarching things like energy systems and psychological implications. As I tried to get more specific, it began to fall apart. It became increasingly clear that science wasn't doing a great job of telling me the best methods – not about running, and certainly not about climbing.

I was looking for answers. For truth.

Years later, Nate and I attended a talk that Eva Lopez, one of the first people to undertake rigorous study on finger strength, gave in Salt Lake City. In attendance was a who's who of coaches and trainers from the area. After she gave a great presentation discussing her own progression as a climber as well as her research and what it meant, she opened the floor for questions. It went something like this:

"So which is more effective, a five-second hang or a ten-second hang?"
"I don't know."
"Is your protocol better than a repeater protocol?"
"I don't know."
"What's the best hangboard protocol?"
"I don't know."
"Your research says that we should do ten-second hangs on a 20mm edge for…"
"No. My research says that for *this* group of climbers, at *this* point in their careers, doing *this* specific protocol was better for them than *this* other protocol. That's it. It doesn't say anything beyond that."
"But…"

These were incredibly smart people. What they wanted from science was immediate answers to every question they could come up with. If science had studied finger strength, it must have the answers, and we should be able to benefit from those answers.

But that's literally not how it works.

I admire Eva's ability to say, "I don't know." It's what science does – and why science exists. In order to study an individual mechanism or action inside of a system with many complex interactions, a researcher needs to control as many variables as possible to try to isolate that individual action. But in the real world, all of those variables – and those complex interactions – still exist. What's more, those researchers are looking for evidence, under the imposed conditions, that either supports or opposes their hypothesis. They are trying to better understand that action so that they can ask further intelligent questions about the interactions. The results will nearly always provide an incomplete picture. So at best, the conclusions we find in any paper should inform our beliefs rather than be taken as the only truth.

When I spoke with movement researcher Rob Gray for the *Expert* series on my podcast, he suggested that when working with athletes, individual case studies might be more applicable than large scale group studies that give us an average or mean result. That group average often represents some mythical average performer but doesn't give you any details about how *individual* athletes actually respond. But those details are important to us as coaches and self-trained athletes. A case study can show us how an individual responds in the lab, as well as how that intervention ultimately affects their real-world performance, something we rarely get from group studies.

To complicate matters even more, because group studies are often looking at isolated actions rather than complex interactions, they are susceptible to missing mechanisms that might be causing their results. It's happened repeatedly:

A 2001 paper from F.-X Li, et al, tried to ascertain whether chalk actually helped climbers gain friction. After all, the use of chalk comes from gymnastics, where it's used to *reduce* friction. They concluded that chalk use wasn't helpful for climbers.

Turns out they were measuring friction in a way that never happens in climbing, and they weren't taking oils from the fingers into account at all. When subsequent studies fixed this error in methodology, the results were more in line with what we already knew: yes, chalk helps (to a point).

A 2009 study from Draper, et al, tried to determine if flexibility is a good indicator of climbing performance. They first asked climbers to get onto a wall and step as high as they could. Next, they asked them to mantle onto the highest foothold that they could. They determined that the best climbers were also the most flexible.

Shown clearly in the photos, climbers were able to lean far away from the wall in order to get their foot higher, placing more of their weight on the seemingly small handholds. Mantling over the high foot would require even more of that strength. Yet no finger or upper body strength was accounted for, and no handhold depth was provided. So yes, better climbers were more likely to do this move, but I can't trust the conclusion that it was due to flexibility.

I'm all for science and the study of climbing. I'm excited about it, actually. It just isn't the vehicle for truth that I once thought it must be, and that many of us still believe it to be.

No matter how much science has looked at climbing, we still don't have the answers. Whenever you see a post on whatever social media app that makes claims about what is best and uses a citation to back up their claims, I suggest you go and read that paper for yourself. It's unlikely the original poster read past the abstract, from which they extrapolated wildly. I doubt they spent time trying to poke holes in the methodology or interrogating the conclusions.

Because they wanted truth. They wanted answers. They wanted science to be right. And it's possible they used that citation as a shield to protect their insecurity about their own credibility.

But we *should* be interrogating and poking holes. It's what science at its best does all the time, to itself.

Yes, of course, there are people out there using citations who are doing it right. There are a lot of valuable studies and thorough researchers, and I'm excited to see where they take things. But you should still check their work. You should check my work. I'm happy to debate my thoughts and they should be too.

And we should all be happy to admit that we don't know.

Changing Constraints Are New Opportunities

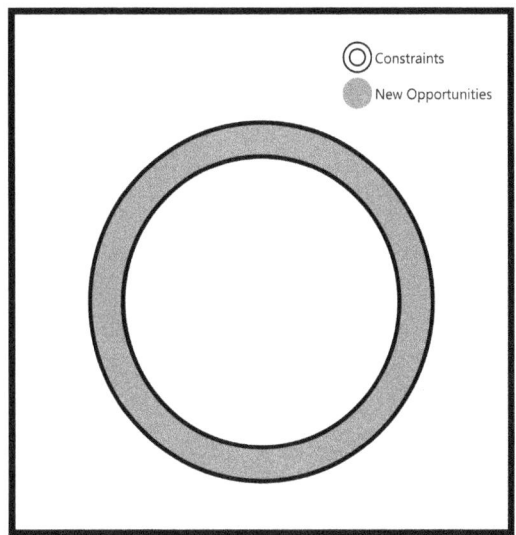

Winter, 2014. I had ticked around sixty 5.13's and had just done my first 5.14. Motivation was high.

Shorter days made the five hours spent driving to the Red a tough proposition. So for me, it was time to train hard and work more hours, making sure I'd have the time off I needed for climbing in the spring.

In 2011 after my grandfather died, we moved into the 492-square-foot house next door to my grandmother, who I called "Mamaw", so that I could help take care of her. It was actually the house she had raised my mom in, and where I had lived for a few years when I was born, but nobody had lived there for the last 30 years. I took time off of work and climbing to completely remodel and transform it from falling apart into a sweet little house that preserved much of its original 1947 character.

But now, three years later, Mamaw was battling cancer, and she didn't seem to have the strength for the fight. I've blocked much of that winter from my memory. Greedy estranged relatives had shown up, and as her power of attorney I was locked in a constant battle with them. She didn't have any money to speak of, but they wanted whatever they could get their hands on. It was exhausting.

My contrarian nature comes from her, and she was quite skilled at finding things to complain about, particularly when people were trying to do things to help her. I probably get that from her as well. But even as she slipped into dementia, she would light up at the sight of my daughter, Katy, who was then 17 and a junior in high school. It made it that much more difficult when, a few weeks into 2015, I had to give Katy the news that Mamaw had died.

That winter, my right shoulder was gradually becoming more and more of an issue. As a mural artist and decorative painter, I spent most of my workday with my arms overhead. Afterwards, I'd go to the gym and climb. For many seasons, the shoulder would be aggravated by the end of the training cycle but then improve throughout the performance season when training volume was much lower. I kept pushing it.

It eventually gave up, spurred on by slipping on a patch of ice at work, landing hard on that shoulder. Imaging revealed that I had completely shredded the bicep tendon that controls lifting the arm overhead, and the fall had finished the job. I'd need surgery to cut out the shredded section and reattach the now-shortened tendon to a different location.

Surgery went well, and my physical therapist, Tammy, was a climber and friend of mine. She understood what I was aiming for, even though her directive through worker's compensation was only to get me back to work. For 30 minutes a day, five days a week, Tammy would help me check the required boxes and then she would turn me loose in the weight room for the remaining 90 minutes of our session.

I was soon feeling stronger and more fit than ever. In an attempt to check in on how my sport climbing skills had atrophied during my time off, I went to The Darkside and got on a 13a I had often used as a warmup during my Swingline campaign. I'd been bouldering in the gym for over a month and felt pretty confident in the shoulder. A 13a I had done more than 50 times should be a good reentry test.

Pumped and nearing the chains, I resorted to a mode that's damn near necessary to climb well in the Red – the "lunge and latch" – when fire shot through my shoulder. I'm not one to catastrophize injury. I've found a way to climb through nearly every tweak or twinge I've felt. But this time, I was worried I had torn the bicep tendon from its new anchor. I hadn't, but I didn't want to push my luck any further.

My motivation to sport climb was dropping. Fast.

Still, I had a goal. What could I do, right at that moment, within these new constraints, to satisfy my goal of becoming the best climber I could be?

I had two choices:
I could work my way through the pain and retrain my brain to understand that it was perfectly safe. It would take time. It would require me to hold myself back from how I like to sport climb.

Or I could go bouldering. So far, bouldering in the gym seemed safe. I would rarely need to go into that pumped lunge-and-latch mode of climbing. I could gradually work my way through difficult, dynamic moves more easily than I could on a rope. And even though what I really wanted to do was sport climb, I knew bouldering was something I needed to do to continue improving.

It was a no-brainer. I set a new checkpoint goal of climbing V10, which seemed impossible at the time.

It was early fall and I couldn't resist getting outside, but instead of going to the crag like I had so many October days before, I drove to the Red and went searching for boulders.

Obviously, I had gone bouldering before. I had even climbed a few endurance V9's in just a few tries. But I hadn't *really* bouldered. I hadn't dedicated time to trying one single difficult boulder. I'd never been invested in it.

Now, because of changing constraints, I was all in.

When bouldering had been just a fun weekend trip, I could justify walking away when something didn't suit me or didn't seem fun to try. I could happily bounce from boulder to boulder with zero agenda.

Somehow, I'd never embraced all that bouldering could teach me. Perhaps, after being maniacally focused during sport climbing seasons, I had needed the mental downtime it provided for those few weekend trips each winter. But now I needed to know what I'd been missing.

What I'd been missing was more opportunities to try a wider variety of moves. Easier access to different styles of climbing. New tactics and the ability to more quickly iterate and learn from subtle changes. More frequent invitations to be more creative. Far more reps at learning to better execute difficult sequences. Bouldering in the gym had provided more of these things when compared to sport climbing, but bouldering outside offered even more than I expected.

I did my first V10 on January 3rd, 2016, eight months after my shoulder surgery. I did two more in the following two months. It was the hardest I had climbed. I was 41 years old, with an 18-year-old daughter, and had spent almost my entire climbing career as a weekend warrior who lived over two hours from the nearest outdoor climbing.

I don't mention these things as obstacles. They were constraints, yes, but constraints simply define the solution space that you're free to explore. It was because of these things that I learned to make the most of a day out climbing. To try harder to get something done efficiently. To be ready when it was time to perform.

But those constraints that had shaped me were about to change.

While workers' compensation was paying me to rehab my shoulder, I had a lot of free time that I could spend at my laptop figuring out how to turn Power Company Climbing into a viable full-time remote business – something that didn't yet exist in climbing coaching. When I eventually returned to my day job, I put in my two weeks' notice.

Shortly after, Katy graduated from high school. With Mamaw gone, she was my only remaining close family, and I knew she would need her own space, both literally and figuratively, to grow into the person she could become. My soon-to-be wife, Annalissa, graduated with her bachelor's in social work and was accepted into a remote master's program. Over the course of a single weekend, we helped Katy open her own bank account, got her a car and insurance, and told her she could move into our house because we were moving out.

In a made-for-TV-movie role reversal, Katy stood in the driveway of our little house, waving and crying as we drove away in my Honda Element to spend a couple of years working remotely and chasing the climbing seasons.

Changing constraints. New opportunities.

EXCEL

- **February, 2019** — *First V11*
- **2019** — *Two 5.13's*
- **April, 2020** — *Granddaughter born*
- **2020** — *Seven double-digit boulders*
- **2021** — *Three double-digit boulders*
- **2022** — *One V10*
- **June, 2022** — *Second daughter born*
- **2023** — *Five 5.13's*
- **2024** — *Fifteen 5.13's*
- **October, 2024** — *One hundredth 5.13 on 50th birthday*

Adapt and Go Boom!

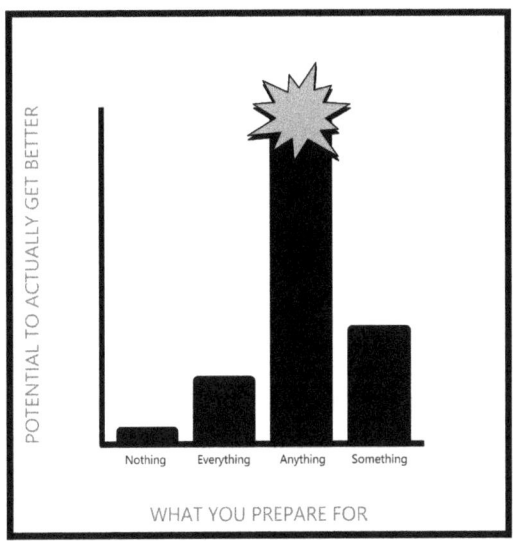

When we think of iconic sport climbing crags, most of us imagine steep, soaring, streaked walls dotted with just enough grips to make possible the rope-stretching pitches. Something like Céuse or Taipan.

Not something like the Rodeo Wave.

The Wave has certainly become iconic, with visitors to Wild Iris often wanting to just go see it. It is very steep, has the same streaks, and a few of its routes do seemingly have just enough grips. But it's tiny in comparison, maybe 50 feet tall and 100 feet wide. Over half of that width is obscured by a giant boulder that sits in front of the wall, about half as tall, and forms a ramp parallel to the angle of the wall. Some of the best routes start off of this boulder and climb barely more than a dozen moves to the top of the wall. Others start in the corridor behind it, requiring effort to only narrowly avoid dabbing. To complicate matters, the routes are so close together that linkups often make just as much sense as the straight up routes. The longest routes take a rising – and sometimes falling – diagonal line across the wall, traversing from the far right to top out on the far left.

What the wall lacks in height, it makes up for in fury. The pockets are farther apart than you want, the feet are worse than you'd imagine, and every move can feel desperate. It's a fantastic compressed test of abilities, and if you reach that level, an amazing outdoor training wall.

Over the years, I've learned to love the Wave, doing all of the 12's and most of the 13's. One route though, Atomic Stetson, a straight up 13c first done by Paul Piana, tested me more than the others.

In Paul's old guidebook, *The Legendary Wild Iris*, his description of the route reads:

> "Pull your hat on tight, step right, off the ramp and go boom!"

In the spring of 2010, after my first blocks of dedicated finger training, I had a breakout Red River season, doing one 13a, seven 13b's (including one in the New River Gorge), and one 13c. So I arrived in Lander that July on our annual trip feeling stronger than ever. In a quick handful of attempts I managed to do Cow Reggae, the 13b considered by many to be a Rodeo Wave rite of passage. That same summer I tried Stetson, the next route to the right. At the time, its bouldery start felt impossible, though I could do the top half without much trouble. During my two-week trip, I never managed to link together any of the first six or so moves.

At the end of the next spring, with a month to train for my return to Wild Iris, I decided to focus on preparing for Stetson. From memory I set a replica boulder at the gym that took a few sessions to link together. By the end of the month, I could do it six times in a row.

On my first day back at the Rodeo Wave I was positive that I was primed for success. I stepped onto the wall, reached to the first mono, and prepared for the next move – which seemed far bigger than I remembered. The holds were more painful and the feet were much worse than my replica's. As I pulled, I felt something shift in my finger. For the rest of the trip, I couldn't pull on monos at all, so Stetson was out.

Over the years, I'd occasionally check in to see where I stood against the bouldery start. Sometimes I could do all but the very first moves. Sometimes it was the final moves before the rest that seemed most difficult. It never lined up to seem feasible.

Then, in the summer of 2019 while I was fully in bouldering mode, my friend and fellow coach Paul Corsaro was visiting and wanted to get the tour of Wild Iris. After a handful of quick sends from 5.12 to 13a, he was feeling ready to check out the Rodeo Wave. I put him on Cow Reggae and sprayed him down the best I could remember.

Since we were there, I figured I might as well check in on Stetson, even though the top was wet. I knew I could manage the climbing up there, but the bottom? I wasn't hopeful. To my surprise, the bottom felt easy on my bolt-to-bolt beta run. I thought I must have somehow skipped something. I tried again and did the entire bottom boulder in one link for the first time.

A few days later I came back and sent, the whole time wondering why it felt so easy.

My interest immediately shifted to the route often called the best on the wall, Atomic Cow. It linked the crux of Atomic Stetson into the crux of Cow Reggae to create a 13d. Capitalizing on this newly discovered ability seemed like the smart play.

At nearly 45 years old it was unlikely that I was physically stronger than I'd been in my 20s and 30s.

What changed?

I hadn't trained for the fingery pockets at all. I didn't quite understand what had happened. On the surface, the route felt so easy that I just couldn't make sense of it.

So I looked deeper.

The way I see it, we can prepare four different ways:

For Nothing.
This is how most climbers "prepare" – by not actually preparing at all. They just go climbing with no intention. They want to be better, but they don't want to do the work to get better. Early on, they'll likely improve this way despite themselves, but that progress will quickly grind to a halt and they'll be in a never-ending cycle, repeating the same "I'm just trying to get back to where I was" session, both indoors and out.

For Everything.
Preparing this way is hectic and usually lacks enough focus to be very effective. Yes, I know you want to be good at steep, vert, slab, crimps, slopers, pockets, bouldering, bouldery sport climbs, long sport climbs, trad climbs, big wall climbing, and more. The problem is, if you prepare to be good at all the things, you're not going to get good at any of them. At best, you'll be mediocre. This can work over a very long time, but it's unlikely you'll improve much while in a constant state of juggling being just ok at so many things.

For Anything.
This, in my opinion, is the best way for most of us to prepare. This is adaptation. It requires constantly pushing up against discomfort, which is, well, uncomfortable, but it's the best way to ensure you have the space and understanding to continue improving. Early on, this method often means doing more and different things. Later in a climbing career, this method

involves finding thematic areas of weakness and exploring them in a variety of situations and scenarios. This is the most robust form of preparation.

For Something.
This type of preparation zeroes in on one specific thing. Training on replicas often fits into this category, as does preparing for a specific grip, say half-crimp, only on a hangboard but never while climbing. Projecting a single climb at the exclusion of other climbing, or climbing on only one angle or style lands here as well. This method can be very powerful for sending if you get it right, and can fill in a skill set if you are already very good at adapting a wide variety of skills. But if you aren't – which is likely the case – or you get the preparation even a little bit wrong, this method quickly becomes very fragile.

I had just begun exploring the movement themes that would eventually become my course, *The Atomic Elements of Climbing Movement*. I realized while climbing with my friend Peter Bonamici that in some positions, he could climb with a level of control that I didn't understand. It wasn't an issue of physical strength. It wasn't a specific hold or position. It was simply an understanding of how or when to create the appropriate tension. I wanted to be able to get into and understand small boxes, and then be able to explode out of them into wide spans. To do that, I was working on understanding and controlling tension at both scrunchy and extended end ranges, and I was getting pretty good at it.

Unlike my earlier preparation for Atomic Stetson, I hadn't worked on a particular move or hold. I hadn't set an imperfect replica and been left unprepared. This time, I had worked across a wide range of grips, positions, and angles, and chosen a variety of projects that would test what I'd been learning. This time, I had worked thematically instead of specifically.

I had built *adaptable* skills and strength, and it was time to capitalize on them.

I started by relearning the 13b, Cow Reggae. Within a few attempts, it felt easy, and became my warmup before trying the entire linkup.

After a few sessions, I was falling at the final hard move of Atomic Cow. Remembering my Swingline and Transworld debacles from years earlier, I made the choice to use my warmup to interrogate my beta for those moves. I wasn't the same me – that was clear – so it was possible I could find a more efficient way to do those moves that played to my new strengths and understanding of movement. I did, opting to get into a small box and make a wide bump move instead of the usual cross.

I hadn't seen anyone use this beta. I only spotted it because I'd become more adaptable in that style of climbing.

Boom!
I sent next go.

Responsibly Selfish

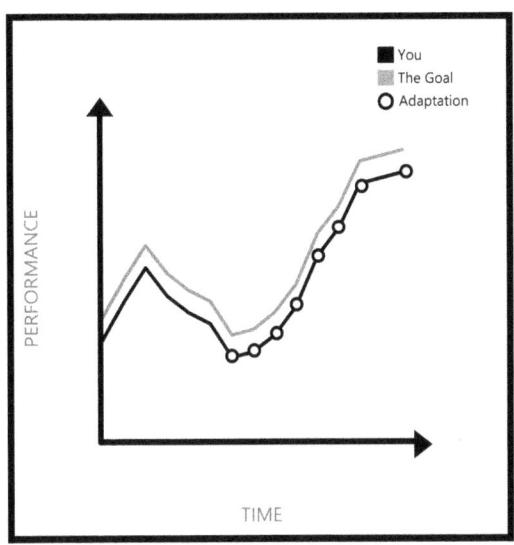

On June 3rd, 2022, I became a father again, 25 years after the first time. At 47 years old, it was going to mean some major life changes that only a few years earlier I hadn't considered would ever be a reality again. The pregnancy wasn't a surprise, so we had plenty of time to prepare.

But I wasn't at all prepared.

My wife is a school counselor, so she had the summer off and was able to take her maternity leave at the beginning of the school year. This gave us plenty of time to be a new little family, but as the golden leaves began to fall from the aspens, she went back to work and I settled into my role as a stay-at-home dad for the remainder of the school year, an opportunity I was lucky to have.
When I was a father the first time, I was only 23 years old, much less patient, and far more self-centered. This time I had the

space and patience to be entirely present for the tender moments. I learned how to make her laugh, watched her figure out how to crawl and put sounds together into words, and got wrapped around her finger. I climbed literally no new things outside that fall. And I didn't for one second wish that I was out climbing.

In early November I started to contemplate what climbing might look like for me going forward. I'd only been bouldering since the start of the pandemic, and at surface level, bouldering seemed like the better option with a baby or a toddler. The problem was that I'd already climbed the boulders I wanted to that would be easy to session with a little one or suitable for a half-day mission. My main climbing partner, Zach Alexander – the kind of partner that makes most others seem inadequate – had moved away at the end of 2021. And finding bouldering partners in Lander was a struggle. Short sport climbing missions when I was free – which would mean very infrequently – seemed like the better option.

But I felt like I needed to find some motivation to get back to sport climbing. Yes, I know the aphorism, "Dedication, not motivation." No, I don't think it's necessarily true, because the two aren't mutually exclusive. In fact, why not use motivation to fuel your dedication? The key is to know how to find the motivation inside yourself rather than relying on outside forces to create it for you. Once you know how to manufacture the motivation you need to reach big goals, it's an undeniable asset.

I do that by throwing my hat over the fence.

I looked back at my sport climbing and realized that I had done over seventy 5.13's. That number seemed astounding, but I wondered if I could reach 100 in the next few years, maybe by my 50th birthday? I knew it would require that I constantly reassess my actual available time and work hard to coordinate with partners, but I also knew I could do it.

If you knew I was trying to reach that goal, it's because you saw me publicly throwing my hat over that fence.

I'd found the new sub goal that would keep propelling me forward. First, I'd have to contend with a finger injury I'd recently sustained while doing some necessary work on my Cincinnati house where my oldest daughter lives. It was a moment of dumb frustration – don't ask. Then I'd need to train. I'd need to learn to sport climb again. And because it's our winter zone here in Lander, I'd have to embrace the vertical, slippery, hateful style of Sinks Canyon.

My office manager, Lana Stigura, had become my regular climbing partner. Partially because schedules were easy to coordinate, but also because she isn't at all afraid to tell me that I'm slacking. She was working on a hard-for-her project in Sinks on a section of wall that had routes at a variety of grades. We rarely ventured away from that wall, and for the first winter back, I didn't even touch a 5.13. Instead, I spent the sporadic sessions I could make time for climbing 5.10, 11, and 12. Some routes I did multiple times, trying different solutions until I could make them comfortable. Then I'd do them again with purposely worse feet, skipping the good holds in the crux, or bypassing the rests. I'd climb them faster, not stopping to chalk. This allowed me to get a huge amount of reps done in a very short amount of time, pushing the boundaries of my discomfort little by little. I still can't say that I love climbing in Sinks, but I learned to appreciate what it could offer, and that's enough for me.

At the same time, I was getting in the gym to try and rebuild the fitness I knew I'd need. As my finger improved, I created a variety of circuits, some easy and some more powerful. Those would make up the bulk of what I did in the gym. Many trainers these days would call it "junk mileage", but I knew I needed to push into the extreme discomfort of being pumped and tired and failing. I'd remember how to stay on the wall, regulate both physically and emotionally, and keep climbing. At the same time, I could avoid the holds that might aggravate the finger.

If that's junk mileage, then I'm all for junk mileage.

The extremely short and sporadic sessions continued until my wife got out of school for the summer. Whenever we could carve the time out, I knew I had to make the most of it and start trying 5.13's. I got a few 13a's and single 13b done, but spent time on a few 13c's which ultimately thwarted my attempts and nearly took up too much of my time.

For the next school year, I knew I needed to get more work done, both on my business and my climbing. We had the opportunity to join a small, newly opened daycare with just a few kids, run out of a friend's house. We opted for two days a week, knowing that the time playing with other kids would be fantastic for our toddler.

With these two days I planned morning podcast interviews and afternoon climbing sessions. I packed those days full of all the things I'd need to get done during the week. This would give me time to work and climb, as well as several days a week to be with my daughter.

That great idea would prove to be a grave error.

As winter moved in, so did every possible illness we could catch. My wife works at the elementary school, so we were living in a very active petri dish. The daycare, which we all loved, got the same sicknesses and needed to close often. Since I didn't need to call anyone to have the day off of work, picking up the pieces fell to me.

Daycare was closed at least one of our days each week for the majority of the winter. This resulted in canceling and rescheduling interviews, sometimes only to have to cancel them again. By the time my voice would recover from Covid or the flu, a new sickness would arrive.

I had to bail on more climbing days than I made it out for, inconveniencing my partners and being forced to sit on the sidelines as I watched my self-imposed deadline creep closer. Somehow, my two main partners that winter, Lana and Cody Kaemmerlen – a recent transplant to Lander and one of the all-time great crag conversationalists – kept climbing with me despite the annoying state of constant flux.

But I still had to contend with myself. I've always prided myself on my work ethic and being a good climbing partner. I also have an innate need to create things, whether they are money-makers or not. These are all inextricable parts of my identity, and they were crumbling.

When I first became a father in 1997, my greatest fear was that I would end up being as terrible as my father had been. But I'm confident that I was a good dad. Now I had a new chance to screw it up, and with everything spiraling, I wondered if I would.

I was unable in the heat of the moment to let go of any responsibilities that winter, neither the mandatory life needs nor those self-imposed. I was going to get the work done. I was going to go climbing. I was going to be a good dad. Even if it killed me.

The reality is that it could have.

For months it felt like I was barely keeping my head above water. I'm not exactly sure where the line is between just being down and depression, but I'd guess I was toeing it. That is, if I hadn't stepped over it entirely.

I somehow managed to get a few 5.13's done in that vertical, hateful Sinks Canyon style, but I was falling way behind – and much deeper into a darkness I'd never experienced. Until something changed, I was going to keep falling.

My wife and I were looking forward to spending the summer traveling with our daughter. I had to tell her that I couldn't do it. I needed time to catch up to myself, and if we left on a trip, it would only stress the system more. I'd made the mistake of trying to optimize my schedule, and when that one thing faltered, the entire system had crumbled.

I needed time to work.
I needed time to climb.

I needed to be selfish.

Selfishness isn't really in my nature. If we're being honest, I tend to shoulder way too much at all times. I suppose that's because I can. But at that moment, I couldn't. I needed to be selfish about my time in order to find the space to climb my way out – both literally and metaphorically. I had to resolidify the identity I'd been building for so many years.

I started by changing the way I think about my business and the social media/content treadmill that seems to be a race to nowhere. I no longer had time to participate in that, so I put my focus on the most valuable content that reached the people who really wanted to hear what we had to say.

I talked with and committed to partners, and did my best to stay in constant contact to know who was climbing where and when. I would plan to try any 5.13's I hadn't done that were near what my friends wanted to climb on. I offered to hang draws, brush holds, work out sequences, or whatever else it took.

Most importantly, I reevaluated where I stood in relation to my bigger goal of becoming the best climber I could be. What could I do right now to make sure I'm not just reaching for more, but also for better?

I wasn't the same me. My ideas about myself and my capabilities had to change. Many of the things that used to be commonplace would require far more effort. I'd have to figure out how to set some things on autopilot that I'd previously afforded time and effort I no longer had to spare.

Life had changed in a lot of big ways, and one thing was very clear:

I needed to adapt.

Quality Control

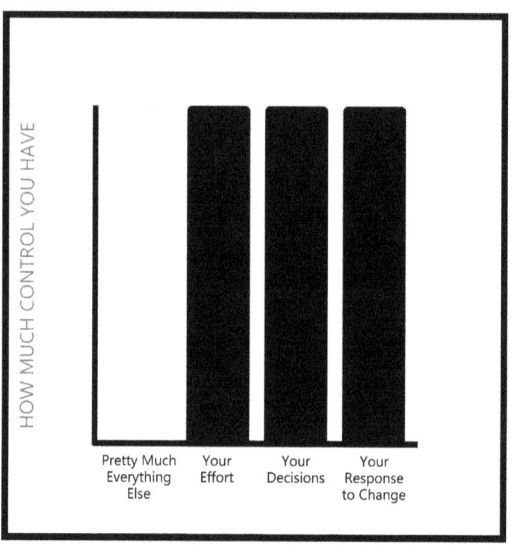

As a coach, I often have to remind athletes of the things that they can and cannot control. We have to keep these things in mind for two reasons:

> So that we don't blame ourselves when we have no control.
> So that we don't make excuses when we are actually to blame.

And of course, all of these possible variables are interconnected and constantly shifting. Even if you have no control over some particular variable, it's possible that you can control a different variable that can change the outcome. For instance, you can't control the weather, but on a rainy day, you can control whether you go to the steep cave that is always dry or try your exposed slab project.

This, my friends, is adaptability.

Rather than a lesson, I just want to give you a list of the things you can control.

Your effort.
Your decisions.
Your response to changing variables.

That's basically it. I'm not saying it's easy. If it were, we wouldn't even be having this conversation.

Comparison Didn't Steal Anything

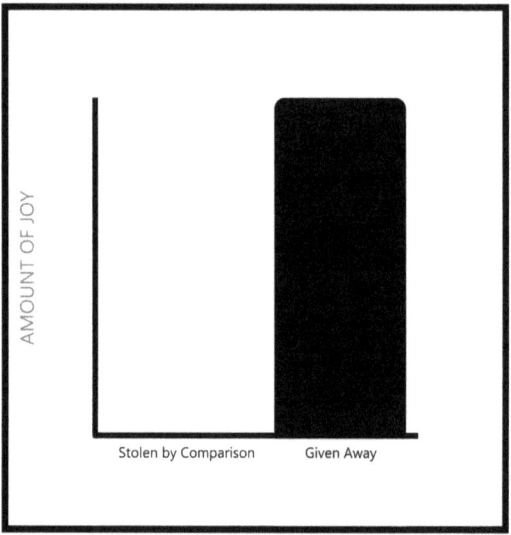

In *The Hard Truth*, I started one of my favorite essays, "No Kings", with a Theodore Roosevelt quote:

> "Comparison is the thief of joy."

Now I'm here to tell you that it's bullshit.

Comparison didn't steal anything from you. If you lost something due to comparison, it's because you willingly gave it away.

At the same time that I came up with this goal to finish 100 routes 5.13 and harder by my 50th birthday, British legend Steve McClure was chasing his 1,000th route 8a, or 13b, and harder.

If comparison was going to steal my joy, this was the perfect opportunity. The number 100 sounded like a lot to me. A nearly inconceivable amount of hard climbing.

But 1,000? Absurd!

My joy wasn't stolen – it was amplified. I became more motivated. The ceiling of possibility had been completely blown off. As an athlete, I want to know where the limits lie. Not because I'm delusional and plan to ever reach those absolute upper limits, but so I can calibrate what might be possible for me.

Soon after setting my goal, I read Steve's book, *Beyond Limits*, as research for a conversation I would have with him for my *Written in Stone* podcast. It was my favorite book of the many I read at that time. Afterward, I spent a lot of time comparing.

Steve and I had very different lives. He'd been a pro climber most of his life, traveling the world in search of the next hard route, while I averaged six to ten days a month outside and had two-week vacations for the vast majority of my climbing career.

Comparison showed me that.

It also showed me how much he loved climbing just for the sake of climbing. How much he revered not only the climbers who paved the way but also the places where we get to play this game.

Me too. Comparison showed me that.

He had set a big but realistic goal that would require him to be dedicated and keep striving to be better. He worked tirelessly within his personal set of constraints to achieve that goal, and now he was closing in on it.

Me too. We had far more in common than not. Comparison showed me that.

Shortly before Steve completed his 1,000th, when he had finished up number 998, he made a post about how it would be a lot for him, but that Spanish climbing legend Dani Andrada had done over 4,600 of the same grade.

Steve was comparing too.

Honestly, I'm not even sure it's possible to avoid comparison. It's a natural human thing. You're going to do it. It's how we engage in and respond to that comparison that really matters.

So choose: you can find inspiration, motivation and awe, or you can give your joy away.

But comparison itself didn't steal anything.

Micro Commitment

Coming out of that eternal winter, I needed a new work project to focus on. I'd spent much of the previous several years reading books and research papers, talking to experts, and experimenting with movement and motor learning. I wanted to know how we learn to move. Not how we *think* we learn. How we *actually* learn.

Seeing how other pursuits had approached the question got me wondering:

What are the fundamentals of climbing movement?

The very base-level building blocks that all movements derive from?

Lots of things are thrown around as fundamentals, but in my opinion, I'd rarely heard a convincing argument that held water.

Over the course of those years, I theorized, experimented, interrogated, and retheorized. Wash, rinse, repeat. Eventually, I came up with a set of fundamentals that I believe form the foundation of every single climbing movement we do. Then I spent over a month creating and testing an evaluation that could help pinpoint which of these fundamentals someone might need the most work on. After filming nearly 50 videos that walk people through the entire system and give them actionable steps towards improvement, I packaged it as a course called *The Atomic Elements of Climbing Movement*.

I also filmed myself completing the evaluation, adding context to the questions and filling in the polar chart that would show my own area of weakness.

The results came back: commitment.

Can't be. I wrote a book about it. I pride myself on my ability to commit.

What I was good at was *macro* commitment. The planning, logistics, and off-the-wall strategies. Throwing my hat over the fence and getting to work while keeping the bigger picture in mind.

But this was different. This was specifically about movement. I had taken my evaluation with a specific scenario in mind: the first or second go on a short-term project, since that's the difficulty I'd be performing at to finish the 100 routes goal. I was honest in my answers, and the evaluation revealed that I was missing a fundamental piece, one I'd overlooked because it only appears in my climbing at this particular level.

Micro commitments.

When faced with a novel move that I wasn't positive I could do, I would balk. It would often take several half-hearted attempts before I stuck it. Standing on terrible feet for a difficult move meant that at best, I would overgrip, and at worst, take several attempts to give a real effort at all. I preferred to stick-clip through and learn the move on toprope before I would fully commit.

These things were slowing down my process, often taking me two or three more attempts simply because I wasn't fully committing to individual moves. Over the course of a sport climbing season, that's a lot of wasted attempts. Wasted days. I didn't have that kind of time to waste.

It was also clear to me that these micro commitments were holding me back from my ultimate goal of being the best climber I could be at any given moment. So I began taking steps toward being more committed. Going for it when I felt uncomfortable. Reminding myself of my goals when I didn't trust a foothold.

I started sending things faster.

Good thing, too, because time wasn't slowing down, my deadline was drawing near, and I would soon end up in a winding detour leading to who-knows-where.

No Time Not To

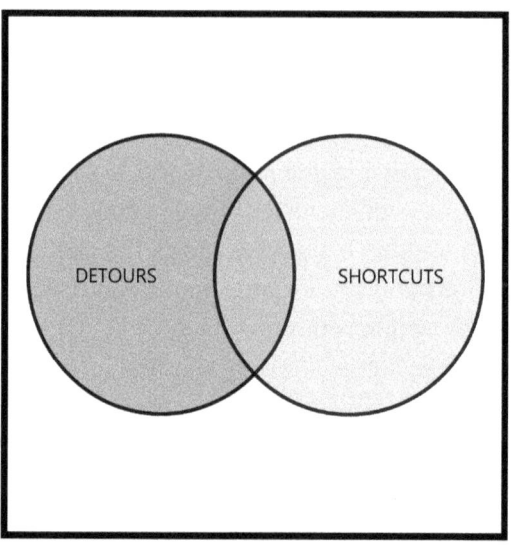

If I was trying to concoct a popular aphorism here, I'd have titled this essay "Detours Are Shortcuts." But we know this isn't true. Detours can be opportunities, as they are essentially changing constraints, but it's rare that they are actually faster.

Rare, but possible, as I'd realize in retrospect. At the time, I thought I was just taking the long way.

In my quest to finish the 100, I was visiting relatively obscure crags and the unchalked (but often quite good) 5.13's that sat dormant there. One of these crags, Miner's Delight, falls into a category that's sadly common around Lander: nearly all-day sun, but impossible to access in the coldest months due to snow. In fact, as I write this, at the end of October, the road to the crag is covered in 18 inches of fresh powder.

Despite this, there were three old 13a's there that I was interested in. One originally done by Steve Bechtel and two by Paul Piana. There were also several unfinished projects, left behind by Paul, Todd Skinner, and Heidi Badaracco, among others.

I don't have the first ascent fever many people are afflicted with. For the most part, I just don't really care who did what first, and my eventual ascent is no less meaningful to me whether I'm the first or the hundredth. But I do appreciate continued significant contributions to the culture of the game we play, and the people who make those contributions. I'd done so many Paul Piana routes in a row that I had taken to wishing myself and my partners "Happy Paul-idays!" On one of those Paul-idays at Miner's Delight, I walked over to check out a panel that held several unfinished projects, including a pair of routes by Todd and Paul.
It was by far the most impressive panel at the cliff, and I was immediately taken by the line Paul had bolted. One hundred feet tall, it resembled a blank and bulging Wild Iris route capped by a steep Red River jug haul. At the juncture of the two sat an obvious crux: a bone white, 15-foot, nearly vertical slab that appeared absolutely devoid of holds.

I had to know what was up there, and why the route hadn't ever been finished.

I didn't intend to get hooked. I was only stick-clipping up on a recon mission. But as I got higher and higher, past clearly possible but difficult climbing, I grew more and more psyched. Then I got to that slab.
Unlike the climbing below me, Paul had cleaned this section, removing the tiny loose flakes characteristic of this rock type. I assume he knew that this section would be the gatekeeper, and if he couldn't crack the code of the slab, there was no reason to continue cleaning the remainder of the route.

There were holds, though I wasn't sure they were usable or close enough to connect together. Immediately after this blank section, the wall kicked back and turned to massive jugs. Those buckets somehow gave me the illusion that it must be possible to get to them. I wasn't sure how, but I was sure it would go. And this route was one of the few that stayed in the shade until about noon.

I left my draws up.

I knew the clock was ticking on the 100, and I knew this wasn't going to be a quick process. It needed a lot of cleaning. A few bolts needed replacing. And there were a lot of moves I was unsure about. Talking people into going there at all was going to be a challenge.

It would be a detour, but one I was sure I wanted to take.

My usual partners were unavailable, but two friends had separately decided to spend parts of the summer in Lander. Ryley Rush, who helps me with *Written in Stone*, our climbing history podcast, and Luke Mehall, who runs *The Climbing Zine*. They both got psyched on the area, and I was eager to take advantage of that windfall.

Taking a cue from Paul, I decided that before I cleaned the top section, I'd spend time on the clearly more difficult bottom. Over the course of three or four sessions, belayed by Ryley and Luke, I worked out a link from the ground all the way to the base of the slab. But I couldn't quite sort out how to connect the few tiny pockets and slopey edges.

Ryley's trip ended. Luke's trip ended. I was no closer, and now I was partnerless with the sound of a ticking clock echoing in my head.

So I threw my hat over the fence.

I spent a few days rapping down the route and cleaning. Replacing bolts. Cleaning some more. Toprope soloing the few moves that blocked my passage. I worked out and then reworked my foot beta. When I couldn't quite make a full-extension move to a hard-to-spot slopey quarter-inch edge, I found a mono-divot to bump off of in exactly the right place.

Tick-tock.

Young and psyched, Jonathan Hörst had begun trying the old Todd project to the right. Jon is the youngest son of Eric Hörst, who I'd known for years through the training world. I'd seen Jonathan grow up, so I was happy to belay him when he sent, giving the crag its first 14a. We then moved over to my project, and for the first time, I linked together the moves on the slab.

It was real. It would go.

I spent a few more solo days cleaning the headwall, digging sand out of hand-swallowing pockets and getting blown around by the epic winds that frequently scour the cliff. I imagined every possible position and removed any tiny loose flakes I might step on. I knew if I ever got here on point that I wanted to be able to blame only myself if I fell off, not the rock.

Tick-tock. Those 5.13's won't climb themselves.

There's a story about Paul in Steve Bechtel's guidebook for the area. As Steve tells it, a famed pro climber had moved to town, and Paul had asked them why they never established new routes.
"I don't have time to do new routes," they said.
Paul replied, "That's funny. I don't have time *not* to."

So I stuck with it.

My friend Jake Dickerson, who had established several classics at Miner's, had an unfinished project there and agreed to go out. I taught Lana how to bolt and she began developing a route. I was getting closer, reworking beta, deciding which bolts to skip, and inching my way to that slopey little edge at the top of the slab.

After one particularly close – but not close enough – attempt, I hung on the rope thinking.

I don't have time to do this route. It might cause me to miss my deadline for the 100, stuck at 90-something and still falling off of this slab. The snow might come and close the roads before I can get it done.

Still, I didn't have time *not* to do this route.

I didn't know it when I started, but working on this route was actually taking me closer to my goal. One very slow, laborious step toward the 100, but leaps and bounds closer to being excited about sport climbing. It was challenging me in a way that forced me to be the best climber I could be, and the test of what I had learned was going to be concentrated to 15 feet of nearly blank, not quite vertical, bone-white dolomite.

I tied in again as the sun began to peek around the corner. The breeze picked up as if on command. The initial crux, a full-extension span to a mono, followed by a powerful gaston move on wishful-thinking feet, went perfectly. I didn't even really need the big rest before launching into the crux panel, but I paused to calm myself.

Skipping the next bolt, I climbed quickly into the slab. As I took the quarter-pad two-finger crimp that would allow me to get a high foot and rock *way* up past the mono-divot to the slopey edge, I glanced at my finger and saw blood dripping from it.

This is it. This is the last try.

I stood up as in-control and tight as I could manage and latched the distant edge. Screaming my way through the insecure slabby exit, with Lana yelling at me to stay on, I knew it was happening.

I swam through 40 feet of overhanging jugs to the base of the final panel. A sequential series of huge moves between two-finger pockets and underclings, finishing on a single giant pocket right at the apex of the cliff, and it was done.

Number 98:

No Time Not To.

It Comes Down to You

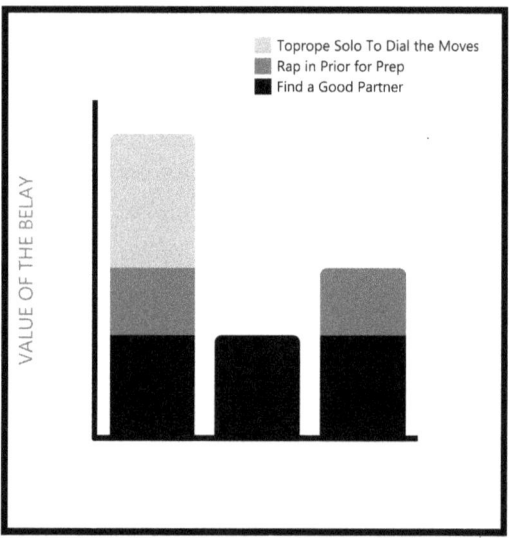

When I talk with climbers who are frustrated about not being able to push their limits, I hear a common complaint:

"Finding reliable partners is hard."

I feel that. But what if I told you that with a little creativity, you can keep working toward your goals *without* partners? That even in sport climbing, how quickly you get things done still comes down to you?

While I was working on No Time Not To and trying to convince people to go out there with me, I began to wonder if it was even possible to reach number 100 with the little time I had left. My wonky schedule wasn't exactly conducive to having regular partners. It had evened out a lot since that winter when everything fell apart, but still the fact that I could only commit to short sessions was a tough sell. People who were off work wanted to do full days, and even when I did find an after-work partner, the time spent driving and hiking often left only enough time for one attempt due to the diminishing daylight of the approaching autumn days. These late sessions also meant I might not make it home in time to tell stories to my daughter as she went to sleep, something I cherish.

Luckily, Cody was still down for quick missions and my friend Leah Scott, who was in and out of town for work, was down for just about anything when she was around. Somehow, sporadic schedules have a way of lining up when people are motivated.

Since I had the ability to get out most days, but only for a few hours at a time, I started looking for ways to use this to my advantage instead of dwelling on the difficulties. As a boulderer, I had spent many solo days working on highballs, either dialing in the bottom or on a rope working out the top. This allowed me to get them done the first time I had a spotter and more pads. I realized I could do the same for sport climbs.

First, I put a short static rope in my truck for rapping down potential routes. I had two dynamic ropes: one cut to Wild Iris-length and one full-length so that I only had to carry as much as was actually needed. I sorted through all of my gear bins to come up with four sets of quickdraws. At some points, all four sets were hanging on various things at different crags so that whenever someone wanted to climb in that area, I was ready.

Many early mornings I would drop Harper off at daycare and then drive out to spend a couple of hours either rappelling down or solo stick-clipping up potential routes in the vicinity of friends' projects. I cleaned several obscure routes that had long been forgotten or ignored. If I thought a route seemed doable with the time I had remaining, and would work with someone else's schedule, I'd hang draws and a fixed line and try it on toprope solo.

This way, when schedules did line up and I could trade belays with someone, I only needed an attempt or two to get it done.

Even though we recognize climbing as an individual pursuit, we often see sport climbing as impossible without a partner. Someone bails and we cancel the entire day. But by breaking it apart and realizing that the early work can be done solo without needing or inconveniencing anyone else, I was able to dramatically speed up the process.

Not to mention, time that I can spend alone while at the same time feeling productive in some way has become increasingly important for me. On these early mornings I rarely saw other people, but regularly ran into herds of elk or other critters I'd likely never see otherwise. I'd listen to the long list of Hip Hop and true crime podcasts I'd gotten behind on. It gave me time to check out new albums, in full, uninterrupted, so that I could later trade notes with my oldest daughter. Or whenever I needed, I could just quietly contemplate.

These solo sessions are a practice I'll continue long into the future, whether I have regular partners or not.

Fold Faster

In 2016, Steven Levitt, economist at the University of Chicago and host of the *Freakonomics Radio* podcast did a large-scale study. He asked people who were facing a tough decision to flip a digital coin, with one side saying "stick" and one side saying "change", and to then follow that advice.

Over 20,000 people participated, many of them contemplating major decisions: 2,200 considering quitting a job; 1,700 trying to decide whether or not to end a relationship; thousands more seeking a randomized coin flip's advice on having a child, going back to school, starting a business, and more.

As you might guess, at the two-month mark, many of the people told to change hadn't followed through, but by the six-month mark, most of those people had decided that they actually *did* need the change. The most surprising result of the study was that the people who followed through with the advice to change were happier, felt they had made the correct decision, and said they'd do it again, as opposed to the people told to stick with their status quo.

Why? Because if they were willing to flip a digital coin and take random advice in the first place, they were ready for that change. They just weren't ready to admit it.

In climbing, we can always try again. And we do, spending season after season on our hardest projects. Getting on, falling off, and getting back on again. It's this kind of constant dance with failure that makes climbing special. But it's also this opportunity to constantly dance that creates our strange relationship with failure.

We don't fail. We try again.

Failure, in climbing, is akin to one thing: *quitting*.

You felt a way when you read that word. It has a negative connotation no matter who you are or how healthy your relationship is with failure. We don't like to quit. We don't want to be thought of as quitters. We don't like to consider what quitting might cost us.

But we'd be better served asking what *not* quitting is costing us.

See, whenever you spend your time on something, it is costing you some other opportunity. Time you could be with family or working on some other route. Time you could be in the gym getting stronger or searching for new boulders. Or a million other things.

This is what economists call "opportunity cost."

What if that other opportunity – the one that you're missing – is worth more to you than the thing you're doing? What if you're ready to flip a digital coin? Doesn't matter. We don't quit.

But we *should*. I had to.

My time was winding down. I still had several 5.13's to do, and at my current pace, there was no way I was going to make it.

Because I hadn't been quitting soon enough.

I drew things out, not wanting to walk away. I should be able to – and probably can – climb just about any 13a. Given enough time, that is. But this was a race. I didn't have the luxury of enough time.

Out here, in the land of very bouldery sport routes with very specific pocket cruxes, it's possible that an easy 13a for someone who's 5'11" will be a low-percentage 13b for me. I can still eke it out eventually, but is it worth the opportunity cost?

In the case of No Time Not To, my answer was yes.
But I'd have to be careful not to make that choice every time.

So, as I was closing in on the goal, but the deadline was closing in faster on me, I set what professional poker player Annie Duke calls "kill criteria."

Annie Duke is also the author of the book *Quit: The Power of Knowing When to Walk Away*. Even though she last cashed in at a poker tournament in 2010, she's still in the top five all-time female money winners, with over 4 million dollars in winnings. You don't get that good at poker by being bad at decision making.

She noticed that people would get trapped in the "sunk cost fallacy": believing that because they had already spent something – time, energy, or money – they had to keep going. They would only look to see what past them had invested and wouldn't ask which choice was better for current or future them. They had money in the pot, they had raised the stakes, and even though they suspected they had a losing hand, they kept playing.

Her answer to stay out of this conundrum herself?
Kill criteria.

She knew that in the heat of the moment, her emotions would influence her decisions. To avoid that, she created a list of criteria that when met, meant she would fold her hand right then and there.

I did the same.

If at any time I felt like injury was a distinct possibility on a route...
I folded.

If I hadn't done all of the moves, and repeated them, by the first attempt of session three...
I folded.

If I regressed on a route in two consecutive sessions, and I couldn't pinpoint something like not getting any sleep or unusually high stress (which rarely crept up two sessions in a row)...
I folded.

If there was a low-percentage move but I could do the remainder of the route, I would give three or four honest efforts. If no send...
I folded.

If I just couldn't get conditions and partners to line up after two or three attempts to do so...
I folded.

Over the past few years, I've seen a growing trend among climbers to create lists of the links needed to send a project, something I've often championed. These lists have the potential to accelerate our progression if we take the simple step of transforming them into kill criteria.

We can do this by adding something Annie Duke calls "states and dates", essentially saying, "I need to be in this state by this date, or I quit."

Notice in my kill criteria, I give these dates as the number of sessions: "I need to be at this point in the project by this session, or I quit." Without this defining factor, these projects could still drag on far too long.

As it got down to the final few days before my birthday and I was still two routes short, I tightened my kill criteria even more. On my first try, I needed to see a strong possibility of doing it that session or the next, or I folded. Often, I wouldn't even go to the top.

My good friend, and one of the best climbing partners ever, Yasmeen, who helped to spark much of this journey, surprised me by coming from across the country to belay me for my last couple of routes. She ended up mostly belaying me on routes that met my kill criteria and got crossed off the list after just one attempt.

But I was crossing them off the list. Narrowing it down. Sooner or later, I'd find one that fit.

Hopefully sooner.

It Ain't Over 'Till It's Over

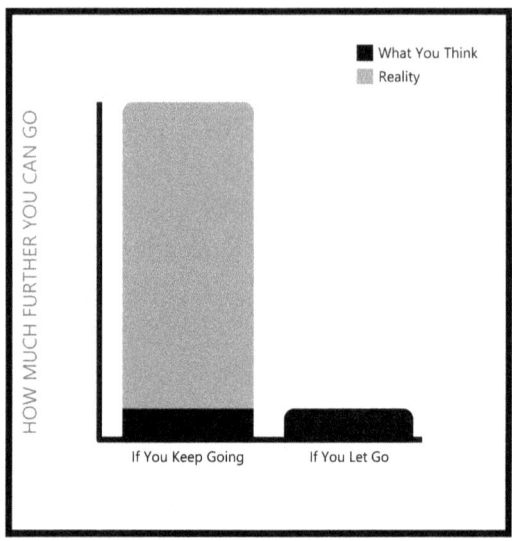

On the morning of Monday, September 30th, I sent out my monthly newsletter, *The Current*. This installment was titled, "I'm Likely To Fail." In it, I wrote:

> "I don't set goals so that I can achieve them. I set goals so that I can chase them. Don't get me wrong; achieving the goal at the last possible moment – the proverbial game winning shot at the buzzer – would be the perfect completion of a pursuit. Because, despite the rhetoric, the outcome is incredibly important. I WANT those 100 routes."

With five days remaining, and two routes left to do, there was still a pretty good chance I could get the 100 done. That evening, Yasmeen and I went to a granite crag just outside of town where there were several 5.13's I hadn't tried.

Granite can be a finicky medium. Technical moves that don't readily reveal their solutions can go from feeling desperate to dialed with a subtle shift of the hips. I wasn't surprised when just sorting out the moves on a line called Awake and Dreaming took far longer than I wanted it to take. However, once I sorted out the four-bolt crux section, I was a little surprised at how difficult the top three bolts felt. The holds were good, but sloping and slippery, and seemed just a little out of my comfortable reach. But this wasn't my first 5.13. I knew I would be able to dial that section in with another go. I had time.

The next morning, we went out to Miner's Delight. Lana would finish up a route she had bolted, and I planned to check out one of Jake's techy 13a's and move a few bolts on another abandoned project near No Time Not To. I was three days on, so I was taking it easy.

On the first pitch of the day, a loose flake was accidentally kicked off that hit Lana and broke her collarbone. We spent the rest of the day getting Lana out of there and to the emergency room. The next day we took her to see a specialist, who suggested surgery.

The goal was no longer a concern. Yasmeen had to fly home. I had three days left, two routes to go, and I felt fine about calling it quits. I figured at best, maybe I'd make it up there to get number 99 done. I'd given it what I could.

I realized there wasn't much I could do for Lana, whose mom had flown in to help out. So early the next morning I went back up to the granite with my toprope solo setup.

I knew there was a 13a there called Broken Heroes that I had avoided due to descriptions of heinous crimps. Accessing the top would be easy, and I could be home by mid-morning.

I didn't find those heinous crimps, but I did find really fun technical climbing. I nearly got up it without falling on my second try.

Now I had numbers 99 and 100 ready to go, at the same crag, with two days left.

As the great philosopher and Baseball Hall of Fame catcher Yogi Berra said:

"It ain't over 'till it's over."

On October 4th, the day before my birthday, schedules lined up allowing me to leverage my already hung draws and promises of good beta to persuade my friends John Wesely and Sean McNamara to go check out the routes. Sean and I both did Broken Heroes in a couple of tries, and moved over to Awake and Dreaming, which I had only been on the one time, four days earlier.

On that one previous go I had worked out the hardest moves to my satisfaction, but I'd made the mistake of not reclimbing the very bottom, which was hard right from the first move. Now, with light fading and thin skin, I psyched myself up for one good attempt. I made it through the bottom and into the hardest moves, barely squeaked my way past a hard crimp undercling, and got set up for what was going to be a desperate cross to a jug.

I lunged… and I fell.

Game over.

I pulled back on and made my way to the top, debating whether or not I should clean the route. I figured I'd be back soon enough, and was at peace with the fact that I might reach the goal a few days late. So I left the draws hanging.

As we were packing up, John suggested that he could come out early the next morning. Sean agreed.

It ain't over 'till it's over.

I had every possible excuse. My skin was thin. I'd be three days on. The route would be in the sun. All true. All factors. But I was going to try anyway.

At 6:15 the next morning, I got a text from John:

"I am up and essentially ready."

And then from Sean:

"My skin is not ready."

I headed out the door. We got to the crag just as the sun was peeking over the horizon, and I went bolt-to-bolt up the route to warm up, dialing in some of the lower beta and making sure I knew the top. Then Sean warmed up doing the same. John took photos.

I was up again. I tied in and calmed myself down. I was confident. The start wasn't perfect, but it felt like it was good enough to keep going. Again, I eked my way through the hardest moves. Again, I fell at the cross.

No worries. I was still warming up. Getting in the right mental space. I had time.

When it was again my turn in the rotation, I felt even more confident. It wasn't too warm yet. I felt surprisingly good for being three days on. This time, I walked the bottom. Everything went exactly right. Again, I fell off at the cross.

Maybe it isn't my day after all.

Sean asked if I wanted to wait a few minutes and give one last effort before it got too warm.

Why not? I thought. *It's likely to be quick.*

I wasn't exactly confident, and if I rested long enough to raise that confidence, the wall would heat up even more and cancel it out. But that doesn't mean I thought I couldn't do it. I knew I could. The chances were low, but there was still some possibility, and any possibility is enough for me to give it whatever I have left.

And that's exactly what I gave.

I didn't float the bottom, but I didn't hesitate. I never even stopped to chalk up. I took every terrible hold as if I owned it. When I got to the cross move where I'd fallen off repeatedly, I didn't second guess anything… and I didn't fall off.

At the jug rest, I felt tired, but the confidence had grown. The next three bolts were considerably easier, and I had worked it out sufficiently. I could do it.

But shortly after I left that jug, I knew I was in trouble.

Staring at the big refrigerator block I had to grapple with, I tried climbing quickly and confidently, though I knew I was fading. That got me through the first move – a huge span off of a slippery edge to a slopey side pull with high, insecure feet. Standard granite sport climbing. However, the fact that I could barely hold the slopey jug afterward was massively amplifying my worry about the next tricky move.

My stance wasn't at all restful, so I tried to keep moving. I didn't complete a single move as I'd planned. At every new body position, I was in a frantic search for kneebars, heelhooks, and anything I could do to take some weight off of my hands. I'd reach around the corner to the small edge, begin to set up for the move, not find the correct position, feel my elbow rising skyward, and go into triage mode, wrapping my leg or my forearm around the corner in hopes of getting some sort of help from the friction. I'd find a brief respite and try again. Several times I moved into position only to clumsily retreat.

At this point the climbing is probably 11a. But the rock was too hot, I was too far gone, and 11a was too hard.

I was positive I was going to fall off, but there was still a tiny percent of a chance I could make it. I wasn't going to fall off without exhausting every option to stay on.

It ain't over 'till it's over.

I eventually found the right combination of position and desperation to commit to the move and fought my way to the dual sloping rails at the top. All I had to do was get a foot up and mantle over. But when I leaned back to raise a foot, I was slipping off.

I had nothing left to hesitate with, so I continued leaning back and falling off, getting my foot up just before my hands left the rail. And then I was standing on top.

Number 100. At the buzzer.
There couldn't have been another attempt.

It threw it all at me. And it nearly knocked me off. I've never been closer to falling without actually falling. But I called on what I had learned from the ninety-nine 5.13's before this one.

I persisted.
I adapted.
I sent.

Then, it really *was* over.

Outcomes Matter: An Epilogue

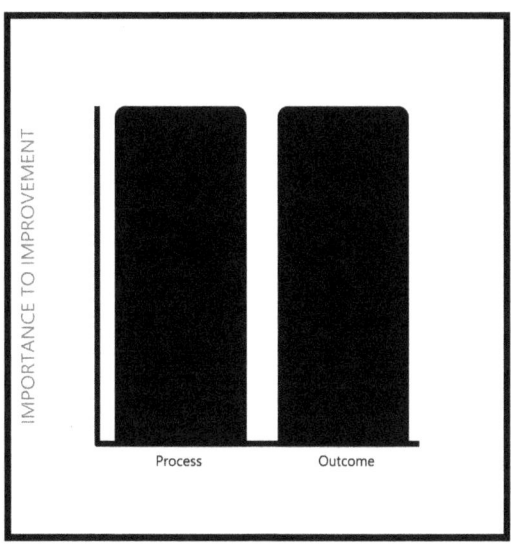

I'm torn.

On one hand, I truly believe that outcomes are important. On the other hand, I try not to place any personal importance on the outcome. If I miss my goal, I'm truly ok with that. It's a data point. That said, one day before the deadline – hell, at the deadline – I'll still be frantically pushing to reach that goal and more nervous as I step onto the wall for that last possible attempt.

I suppose this is a struggle as old as time itself.

I'm willing to entertain the idea that maybe I should spend more time celebrating my achievements. I mean, if I set goals that will ultimately require a personal transformation, the outcomes have to be more than just a data point about the effectiveness of the process, don't they?

Here's the question that rattles endlessly in my head:

> *If the outcome is a data point reflective of my process, and my process is, ultimately, in service of improving myself, what does a failed outcome mean about me as a person?*

I know I shouldn't take it personally. It's all an experiment, so I'd be better served if I could look at it as a scientist: take it seriously but not personally. I wrote about this in *The Hard Truth*, but it's easier said than done. I should probably read it again.

I'm getting older and I have no idea how much time I have left in this game. I didn't set a finish line because it's a lifelong pursuit. But there is a finish line. It's been set for me, and right now I have no idea where it is. That sounds terrifying, but I mostly see it as freeing.

I'm also not sure I've truly learned my lesson about trying to do too much. To be honest, I'm not sure I want to learn it. Or maybe I've learned it but don't really care. A big part of me would rather risk digging myself into a hole than not try to do more. I'm sure there's a middle ground to find, and maybe someday I'll find it. For now, though, I'll keep interrogating myself, keep asking if I'm the same me, and keep adapting, even when – especially when – things get hard.

My joy truly comes from the formation of a goal, and even more so, from the act of chasing that goal and all its checkpoints along the way. It comes from the learning required. It comes from the poignant failures that show me exactly what I'm missing. This means I'm free to follow the detours, even if they don't turn out to be shortcuts, because I can always double back. I'm free to make the wrong decisions because I can do my best to correct them. I'm free to continue setting new checkpoints as long as they lead me toward being the best I can be.

And I will, of course. One more 5.13 will put me at 16 in 2024, the most I've climbed in a year, so I'll probably aim first for that. There are unfinished things I bolted on days I had no partners, and more lines I'd still like to explore. There are harder things I'd like to climb. A climbing wall to build for my daughter. There are more creative ways I want to engage with the climbing community – courses, podcasts, and videos.

There's never a lack of potential checkpoints, only a lack of time to actually reach them.

Through it all, I've dreamed. I've tried. I've made mistakes and tried again. I've asked why. I've learned a lot of lessons. I've adapted.

When I finally do arrive at the finish line, I'll have done enough to feel like the outcome is a positive one.

That much, I'm not torn about.

COUNT TO 100

YEAR	ROUTES		BOULDERS		SIGNIFICANT EVENTS	COUNT TO 100
2005					Started endurance training.	0
2006	30	5.10			Learned to sport climb outside.	0
	11	5.11				
	2	5.12a				
2007	50	5.10			First 12a, 12b, 12c onsights.	1
	85	5.11				
	62	5.12				
	1	5.13a				
2008	45	5.11	6	V6	Added indoor bouldering to training.	12
	61	5.12	7	V7		
	9	5.13a	1	V8		
	2	5.13b				
2009	24	5.12	6	V6	Added finger training; moved all on the wall training to boulders.	20
	3	5.13a	7	V7		
	3	5.13b	1	V8		
	2	5.13c				
2010	19	5.12	9	V7	Started first long-term projects.	34
	2	5.13a	3	V8		
	11	5.13b	1	V9		
	1	5.13c				
2011	7	5.12	3	V7	Took fall and winter off from outdoor climbing.	39
	2	5.13a	1	V8		
	2	5.13c	4	V9		
	1	5.13d				
2012	11	5.12	1	V7	Took off early winter from outdoor climbing. First 13a flash.	52
	5	5.13a	1	V8		
	6	5.13b				
	2	5.13d				
2013	17	5.12	7	V7	Spent a lot of time projecting 5.14a.	61
	1	5.13a	2	V8		
	6	5.13b				
	2	5.13c				
2014	22	5.12	1	V7	First 13a onsight.	67
	3	5.13a	1	V9		
	2	5.13b				
	1	5.14a				

Year	#	Route	#	Boulder	Notes	Total
2015			3	V7	Shoulder surgery in April.	67
			2	V8		
2016	20	5.12	8	V7	Took first extended road trip. Second 13a flash.	74
	3	5.13a	1	V8		
	4	5.13b	1	V9		
			3	V10		
2017	10	5.12	4	V7	First V10 outside of the Southeast, in Hueco Tanks. Moved to Lander.	76
	2	5.13a	4	V8		
			4	V9		
			1	V10		
2018	17	5.12	6	V7	Suffered first major finger injury that prevented climbing.	78
	1	5.13a	1	V9		
	1	5.13b				
2019	7	5.12	5	V7	Focused on bouldering.	80
	1	5.13c	8	V8		
	1	5.13d	5	V9		
			1	V10		
			1	V11		
2020			8	V7	COVID-19 pandemic. Focused on finding and developing new boulders.	80
			5	V8		
			4	V9		
			6	V10		
			1	V11		
2021			9	V7	Focused on finding and developing new boulders. Many first ascents.	80
			5	V8		
			4	V9		
			2	V10		
			1	V11		
2022			2	V7	Daughter born in June.	80
			2	V9		
			1	V10		
2023	6	5.12			Returned to sport climbing.	85
	4	5.13a				
	1	5.13b				
2024	11	5.13a			Sent route #100 of 5.13 and harder on 50th birthday.	100
	3	5.13b				
	1	5.13c				

ACKNOWLEDGEMENTS

While the experiences in this book span a timeframe of roughly 20 years, the idea to make the book didn't actually arise until after I finished number 100. To get it out as quickly as we did was a herculean effort. Once I'm all in on doing a thing, I tend to forget that. So before I go any further, I have to thank Lana Stigura for not only all of the belays during that terrible winter, but also for sitting across from me and helping to get this book out under pressure and pushing to make it better.

On the surface, it could seem like there were 100 belays that should count for this project. But the reality is that there were thousands. Sends of lower grades and failures on harder grades. They all mattered. Thanks if you were one of those.

If you were mentioned in this book, it's because you were more than a belayer. You were or are a partner, and I don't take that lightly. I'll accept belays from a lot of people, but if I'm being honest, I'd rather it were you.

To the people who went out of their way to help me reach this checkpoint, thank you. You didn't have to. I owe you, and I mean that. You get a big assist. Let me get one too.

I try to constantly better myself, in part, because people are paying attention, and I hope to be a positive example. Thanks for paying attention.

The people I most hope to be a good example for are my girls: my wife, my daughters, and my granddaughter. I really don't know how I got so lucky.

ABOUT THE AUTHOR

As the owner and founder of Power Company Climbing, Kris has written training plans for thousands of climbers all over the world. He hosts several successful climbing-themed podcasts, his musical background informing his creative story-telling style. His interest in physical puzzle solving started in his youth with skateboarding and gymnastics, where he also eventually discovered his interest in teaching.

    He started climbing in a Cincinnati gym in 1995 and was quickly seduced by the grand stories of traditional climbers. After a break of several years to focus on music and parenthood, he returned as a dedicated sport climber. At 40, he climbed his first 5.14 and then abruptly switched to bouldering. Age 44 brought his first V11, and 48 brought another daughter, at which point he rededicated himself to sport climbing in his new home of Lander, Wyoming.

    He knows he did the whole thing backward, which is just as well since even though he is an actual Papaw, he's still doing his best to avoid the old-folks endurance retirement home where all of the residents wear matching knee-pads.

www.ingramcontent.com/pod-product-compliance
Lightning Source LLC
Chambersburg PA
CBHW061748070526
44585CB00025B/2828